The
Ladies Aid
Cookbook

BEATRICE VAUGHAN

THE

Ladies Aid

COOKBOOK

Recipes from a Great Tradition of
Fine Cooking, Collected & Presented
as a Family Cookbook for Everyday Use

By BEATRICE VAUGHAN

ILLUSTRATIONS BY JOHN DEVANEY

The Stephen Greene Press

BRATTLEBORO, VERMONT

This book has been produced in the United States of America: designed by R. L. Dothard Associates,

It is published by The Stephen Greene Press, Brattleboro, Vermont 05301.

Library of Congress Catalog Card Number: 77-148619
International Standard Book Number: 0-8289-0125-2

Contents

In this book I've assembled recipes for some of the good food that I've encountered over the years at sales, suppers and bazaars. Since I obviously couldn't include the rules for all the delicious offerings, I've chosen those that particularly appealed to me, some a bit unusual, all superb cookery. For those looking for more strictly basic recipes and traditional dishes, I suggest my earlier books, *Yankee Hill-Country Cooking* and *The Old Cook's Almanac*. And for those looking for specialized recipes using particular New England foods, there are my three smaller books, *Store-Cheese Cooking; Real, Old-time Yankee Maple Cooking* and *Real, Old-time Yankee Apple Cooking*. B.V.

To the Ladies

I like to think that as soon as two families had settled down in new homes in the wilderness, the womenfolk started working together in their own small "ladies aid" society. They may never have called their efforts that in just those words, but the purpose was there, nevertheless. And the goal was identical to that of countless women's auxiliaries all over the world today.

Community betterment almost always takes money. Long ago women had little cash and ways to raise it were few. So they turned to the products of their own hands—sewing and baking, knitting, crocheting, and preserving. I'm sure that even in those early years the industrious ladies were well aware that nothing found such a ready sale as the good things cooked in their own kitchens. Today, food is still a prime source of the funds of any women's society, whether from a supper, food sale, Christmas Bazaar or Dime-a-Dip luncheon.

For hundreds of years these women have sewed and knitted and baked. In towns all over the nation a small library, an enduring church, a preschool clinic, or neighborhood park all stand as silent monuments to the industry and devotion of the ladies. It matters not at all whether a group be called the Auxiliary, Ladies Aid, Altar Society, Sisterhood, Circle or Guild. All were formed for but one purpose—making their communities better places in which to live.

Menfolk have often poked gentle fun at their fund-raising women, but eyes have nonetheless betrayed their pride. Husbands have pretended to scoff at putting on a supper to raise the remainder of the minister's salary, but, underneath the little jokes, they paid silent tribute to the dollars transferred next day to the church treasury.

My father used to complain loudly whenever another supper was in the offing. "All nonsense!" he'd declare. "If everyone turned in a couple of dollars and stayed home, you'd come out just as far ahead." Or he'd argue: "It's just taking money out of one pocket and putting it in another."

Perhaps there was more than a little truth in his complaints. After all, the women gave the food, cooked it, served the supper and washed the dishes while their families came and paid money to eat that same good food.

But Mother patiently explained to Father over and over again, "It's the only way you *can* do it. Folks just won't pay out money unless they're getting something they can see for their dollars."

Over the years, the customers of thousands of such affairs have had their money's worth in full measure. For it is my considered opinion that the members of women's groups of whatever name in whatever town are among the best cooks in the whole surrounding countryside. Each lady painstakingly cooks her specialty and proudly contributes it to food sale or supper.

It may be a traditional dish, the "receipt" handed down in her family for generations and carefully updated. Or it may be a brand new recipe, an innovation made possible by the new and wonderful products available today for modern kitchens. But when you sit down at a long table in a community center or church vestry, or buy some delicious cake, pie or candy on the village green, you can be very sure that you're sampling the best food to be found for miles around.

Often when we're traveling through a little town, we see a big banner hung across the main street, telling the public that a chicken pie supper is scheduled for that night and all are welcome. It will be worth the while of any motorist in not too much of a hurry to break his journey at such a spot and enjoy the wonderful home-cooking of that area.

Many friendly women have written me in the years since my *Yankee Hill-Country Cooking* was published. Many of these warm-hearted letters have told me about dishes popular in their areas. And some speak of the way in which their own particular group is raising funds for a pet project.

Nor is the good work of women's auxiliaries confined to any particular region. A New England friend told me that while traveling abroad she has made a beeline for a food and handwork sale put on by Dutch Navy wives and felt "right back home" at a parish bazaar outside London. From a cousin in Nova Scotia I learned that her group there and its projects are very like ours here. My Ohio sister-in-law tells me of the work of her Circle, no different from that of our Ladies Benevolent Society in Vermont and Women's Society in Florida. Not long ago I listened to a retired minister talk of his years with a church on the Omaha Indian Reservation in Nebraska. And sure enough, an active Ladies Aid Society was there, too.

The range of projects embraced and supported by our auxiliaries is wide. It may be a new carpet for the church, as was ours recently in Thetford, Vermont. It may be funds to send a crippled child or two to a summer camp as we did in Tangerine, Florida. Or it may be a most ambitious project indeed for a local hospital or a new firehouse or a community center, involving fund-raising for several successive years.

Without the Ladies Aid and its sister organizations over the years since this country was young, communities would have been poorer places. Without these clever ladies, good cooks all, the whole world would be a far less pleasant place.

And to every woman who has ever peeled a bushel of potatoes for a supper, baked half a dozen pies for a food sale, then stood on tired feet on a hot August afternoon to sell them, this book is affectionately dedicated.

Bea Vaughan

East Thetford, Vermont
Mount Dora, Florida

Farm Pea Soup

(Eight servings)

1 pound green split peas	pinch of pepper
2½ quarts cold water	3 medium onions, chopped
1 leftover meaty ham bone	3 medium carrots, chopped
½ teaspoon salt	1 large stalk celery with top, chopped

Wash peas, cover with the cold water, and let stand overnight. Do not drain: turn peas and water into a large kettle. Add ham bone (there should be at least ¼ pound of meat left on the bone) and salt, pepper and vegetables. Cover and simmer for 2 hours over very low heat. Remove the bone and pick off the meat, dicing it. Continue cooking the soup over low heat for another hour, then put through a coarse sieve or whirl a few seconds in a blender. Return to heat and add diced ham. Add additional salt, if necessary. Heat very hot and serve. Can be re-heated successfully.

Hearty and good. The flecks of orange carrot and bits of ham add to the attractive appearance.

Temptress

The utmost ingenuity is called for when a neighbor is ailing and nothing seems appealing to a capricious appetite. Father expressed it bluntly. I remember him saying: "May W—— is off her feed, so Mother's been in the kitchen all morning stirring up something that will strike May's fancy."

Chicken-Clam Soup

(For four)

2 cups chicken broth
1 chicken bouillon cube
1 tablespoon melted butter
1 tablespoon flour
1 (7-oz.) can minced clams,

undrained
½ cup milk
½ cup light cream
¼ cup shredded cooked chicken
meat

Heat broth to boiling point and add the bouillon cube, stirring to dissolve. Combine melted butter and flour smoothly, add hot broth gradually, and stir over low heat until smooth and thick. Add undrained clams, milk, cream and chicken. Heat very hot, but do not boil. The flavor is improved if allowed to stand for ½ hour over very low heat.

Old-fashioned Scrap Soup

(Six servings)

2 cups scraps
5 cups water

salt and pepper to taste
bouillon cubes, if desired

This is one of my favorites, if properly prepared. It is a cousin of the thrifty French cook's perpetual soup pot. The scraps may be the combination of a few lettuce leaves, celery tops, a bit of meat or spoonful of leftover vegetables, a chop bone, a scrap of fish, an end of raw onion, any leftover that doesn't seem to have an immediate use. Store all scraps carefully in the refrigerator until you have enough to make soup. And don't forget that a spoonful of leftover cereal is good soup material, too.

Simmer the scraps and water for about 1½ hours. If you have no meat or bones to use, try adding two or three bouillon cubes for additional flavor. Remove bones from soup and whirl it in a blender or put through a sieve. Season to taste with salt and pepper and serve very hot.

Cream of Corn Soup

(For six)

3 tablespoons melted butter or margarine	1 teaspoon salt
	small dash of pepper
1 small onion, peeled and diced	3 cups milk
3 tablespoons flour	1 (1-lb.) can cream-style corn

Simmer the butter and onion for about 5 minutes: do not allow the onion to brown. Blend in the flour, salt and pepper. Add 1 cup of the milk and stir over low heat until smooth and thick. Add the remainder of milk, and the corn. Whirl in blender or put through coarse sieve (the blender does a beautiful job on this soup). Heat very hot, but do not boil.

Lentil Soup

(For eight)

1½ cups dried lentils	½ teaspoon seasoned salt
7 cups water	pinch of pepper
½ cup diced onion	2 cups undrained canned tomatoes
½ cup diced celery	2 beef bouillon cubes
¼ pound ground salt pork	

Wash lentils and cover with 7 cups of water. Add onion, celery, salt pork, seasoned salt and pepper. Cover and simmer until lentils are tender, about 1½ hours. Add tomatoes and bouillon cubes. Continue simmering for 30 minutes longer. This may be served at once, but is more delicious if allowed to stand over very low heat for an hour or so. The heat should be just enough to keep the soup hot, but not high enough to cook it any further.

A robust soup, thick and brown. It reminds me of old-fashioned baked bean soup.

Country Style Onion Soup

(Six servings)

1 envelope dry onion-soup mix   1 cup light cream
4 cups boiling water   grated Parmesan cheese

Combine soup mix and boiling water, cover and simmer for 10 minutes. Add cream and stir to mix. Heat very hot but *do not boil,* or the soup will curdle. Serve at once with grated Parmesan cheese sprinkled over each serving.

Quickly made, with a dark creamy color and fine flavor.

Cream of Potato Soup

(Four good servings)

1 medium onion, peeled and diced   1 tablespoon butter or margarine
2/3 cup water   1 chicken bouillon cube
1 cup seasoned mashed potato   salt and pepper to taste
2 cups milk   grated Parmesan cheese
1/4 cup cream

Cook onion and water, covered, until onion is very tender. Remove from heat and stir in mashed potato, then put the mixture through a sieve or whirl in a blender. Add milk, cream, butter and bouillon cube; heat very hot but do not boil. Season to taste with salt and pepper, serve with the Parmesan cheese sprinkled over each portion.

This soup is improved if allowed to stand a few hours for flavors to blend. It can be refrigerated and re-heated with good results. After standing, the soup may thicken to the point that a little more milk may be added.

Ground for Complaint

My grandfather was a great meat-eater and wanted it on the table three times a day, but he had no use at all for lamb or mutton; and of all mutton dishes, he detested mutton soup the worst.

When Lizzie Borden wielded her axe in 1892 in Fall River, Grandfather read every word the Boston newspaper printed about the case. He declared after it was all over that, if Lizzie had been found guilty, the verdict would have been justifiable homicide. "Do you know what Mrs. Borden served her family for breakfast that morning—right in the hottest August dog days, too? Cold mutton soup, that's what. Cause enough for murder, I should judge."

Easy Vichysoisse

(Four servings)

1 (14-oz.) can chicken broth
1½ cups diced cooked potatoes
1 tablespoon diced onion
1 teaspoon salt
small pinch of pepper
1 cup dairy soured cream
chopped chives

Put all ingredients except the soured cream and chives in the blender, cover and whirl at high speed for about 8 seconds. Add the soured cream and blend for another 8 seconds. Chill well for at least an hour. Serve with chopped chives for garnish.

Best Oyster Stew

(Two big servings)

2 tablespoons butter or margarine
½ pint fresh oysters, undrained
1 cup clam broth (canned is fine)
pinch of salt
small dash of pepper
1 cup rich milk
additional butter, salt and pepper, if desired

Melt butter in heavy skillet. Pick over oysters to insure no bit of shell remains; add oysters to the butter. Add clam broth, salt and pepper, and simmer over low heat for 10 minutes. Add the milk. Heat very hot but be sure the stew does not boil. Taste and add more salt and pepper, if desired. A small bit of butter may be added to each individual soup bowl. Pour hot stew into each bowl and serve at once.

The best oyster stew you'll ever eat!

Grandmother's Table

Grandmother Emerson was a famous cook in our community, and Grandfather never had any trouble getting harvest crews to come to his place. But my grandmother had one inflexible rule: her food wasn't to wait on anyone—when she rang the dinner bell from the shed doorway, that meant dinner was on the table.

Her food was so good and her rule so adamant that one hired man expressed it this way: "When Jen Emerson calls us to eat, we just leave our hoes hanging right in the air."

Brunswick Stew

(Eight to ten servings)

½ medium (*c.* 2½ lbs.) frying chicken
½ pound stewing beef, cubed
2 medium onions, peeled and sliced
1 teaspoon salt
pinch of pepper
3 cups water
1 (8-oz.) can tomato sauce
1 (1-lb.) can whole kernel corn, undrained
1 (1-lb.) can baby lima beans, undrained
1 large potato, peeled and diced
¼ cup rice
1 tablespoon Worcestershire sauce
3 drops Tabasco sauce
3 tablespoons butter or margarine
¼ cup dry breadcrumbs

Place chicken, beef, onions, salt, pepper and water in a large, heavy kettle. Cover and simmer until the chicken meat is ready to leave its bones. Remove chicken from the kettle and cool, then pick the meat from bones and skin. Cut the chicken meat in pieces and return to kettle. Add tomato sauce, vegetables, rice and sauces —all except butter and crumbs. Cover and simmer about 2 hours (the longer it simmers, the more flavorful the stew, so use the lowest setting of the burner that will keep the stew just gently simmering). During the last ½ hour of cooking, add butter and crumbs. The stew should be very thick, and the crumbs help thicken it. Makes about 3 quarts. Serve very hot in soup plates, with hot bread and butter.

This is "Burgoo," a complete main dish that is even better when warmed-over.

Clam Chowder

(For six)

¼ cup diced fat salt pork	2 (7-oz.) cans minced clams
1 small onion, diced	3 cups milk
2 medium potatoes, diced	½ cup light cream
1 cup boiling water	salt and pepper to taste

Cook diced salt pork in a small frying pan over low heat until golden, but be sure it does not get dark brown. Add onion and simmer for 5 minutes. Cook diced potatoes in the water until just tender; do not drain. Add salt pork and onion to the potatoes and water, including every bit of pan fat. Add undrained clams, milk and cream. Add salt and pepper to taste. Cover and let stand over very low heat for about 1 hour in order that flavors may blend. Care must be taken that the heat is not too high or chowder may scorch or curdle. Serve very hot with pilot crackers.

This good chowder is even better re-heated the second day.

Conditioned Reflex

Some of the older women had never in their entire lives eaten at a restaurant or other commercial eating place. And when they went to community suppers, they had no time to sit down at the tables but were content to snatch a few mouthfuls on the run between stove, dining room, and sink as they did their share for Waiting-on-Table or Clean-up. And when they traveled down to White River Junction every fall for a day at the big Connecticut Valley Fair, they invariably ate in the big tent that housed the dinner operations of the Methodist Women. It was considered eminently respectable to be seen in that tent or in any of the others run by a women's group.

But these were so nearly identical to community suppers at home that Mrs. T—— once got up absent-mindedly after she had eaten, stacked her dishes, and headed for the rear of the tent where the dishes were being washed.

Vegetable-Cheese Chowder

(For six)

2 medium potatoes, peeled and diced	4 tablespoons melted butter or margarine
2 medium carrots, peeled and diced	
1 medium onion, peeled and diced	4 tablespoons flour
2 large stalks celery, sliced thin	1¾ cups milk
1 teaspoon salt	2 cups shredded sharp cheddar cheese
1¾ cups water	1 (1-lb.) can cream-style corn

Cook vegetables in the salted water for 15 minutes. *Do not drain.* Blend melted butter and flour smoothly, then add the milk, stirring over low heat until smooth and thick. Add cheese and stir until melted. Add corn to the undrained vegetables, then add the cheese mixture. Heat very hot, but do not boil, and serve.

We like this served with bread and butter instead of crackers. I have a more streamlined version of this very hearty soup in *Store-Cheese Cooking.*

Tomato Soup French Dressing

(About 3 cups)

1 (10½-oz.) can condensed tomato
    soup
1 cup vinegar
½ cup salad oil
1 tablespoon Worcestershire sauce
2 teaspoons salt

⅔ teaspoon paprika
⅓ teaspoon pepper
1 teaspoon ground mustard
¼ cup sugar
1 tablespoon grated onion
2 garlic cloves, peeled and halved

You will need a quart glass jar with tightly fitting lid. Pour soup, vinegar and salad oil into the jar, then add remaining ingredients in order. Replace jar cover and shake vigorously. Chill for 24 hours before using so flavors can blend. Shake before serving.

One of the most satisfactory all-purpose dressings that I know. It has been a great favorite of Supper Committees for its ease of preparation and its low cost.

Celery Seed Salad Dressing

(About 3 cups)

1 cup sugar
2 teaspoons dry mustard
2 teaspoons salt
2 teaspoons paprika

½ cup vinegar
2 cups salad oil
1 tablespoon grated onion
2 teaspoons celery seed

Combine first five ingredients. Stir to mix well, then add the oil very slowly, beating well with electric beater. Stir in the onion and celery seed. Store in covered jar in refrigerator and let stand 24 hours before serving to allow flavors to blend.

This is one of the best dressings I know, rather sweet and attractively colored. It's excellent for all green salads. I make this in my blender, which does a marvelous job.

Onion Salad Dressing

(About one pint)

1 tall can evaporated milk	¼ cup catsup
1 envelope dry onion-soup mix	½ teaspoon Worcestershire sauce
½ cup vinegar	⅛ teaspoon Tabasco sauce

Combine all ingredients in a jar. Cover tightly and shake well until blended. Let stand several hours before serving.

This tangy dressing is about the consistency of Russian dressing and is wonderful on tomatoes, cucumbers, hearts of lettuce, etc.

"Every First Wednesday"

The regular monthly meeting of the Society is the hub around which the whole organization revolves. Nowadays, these meetings are apt to be afternoon affairs. Years ago, however, they were often all-day meetings. Sometimes, too, when the membership was largely composed of mothers of young children, meetings might be held in the evening when fathers could act as baby-sitters; and the session would end with a before-bedtime supper whose richness and variety seemed likely to court an uneasy night.

But whether a luncheon, afternoon tea or evening snack, all hostesses prided themselves on achieving both quality and quantity. The test of accomplishment was to have guests say afterwards, "Never tasted better vittles in my life than Miz' P——set on her table for the meeting." Or, of some unlucky hostess a humiliating criticism might be heard, such as, "My stomach didn't set a bit good, after. M—— B—— always did have the name of a 'greasy' cook."

For many a woman, the monthly meeting was her one and only purely social outing. Each month she tasted other women's cooking and caught up on her "visiting." And she was expected to be hostess when her time came, barring some unforeseen catastrophe, for it was a matter of pride for each to take her turn at entertaining, putting both her house and her cooking on the line, so to speak.

Blender Mayonnaise

(About 1¼ cups)

2 egg yolks or 1 whole egg   2 tablespoons vinegar
½ teaspoon ground mustard   1 cup salad oil
1 teaspoon salt

Turn egg yolks, mustard and salt into the blender. Add the vinegar and ¼ cup of the oil. Cover and turn the blender on at high speed for 1 second. Uncover and add the remaining oil very gradually, the blender turned to high speed. Turn off blender at once when oil is all used. Store mayonnaise in a covered jar in the refrigerator until served.

Creamy Salad Dressing

(About 2½ cups)

1 teaspoon dry mustard   1 egg, to be beaten in
1 teaspoon salt   1 can sweetened *condensed* milk
1 cup vinegar

Combine mustard, salt and vinegar. Add the egg, beating it in well with a rotary beater. Stir in condensed milk and beat to mix thoroughly. Cook over hot water, stirring constantly, until thickened. Cool before using.

Much like old-fashioned boiled salad dressing, it's excellent for potato salad or cole slaw.

Quick Creamy Dressing

(About 2½ cups)

1 pint commercial mayonnaise or   ½ cup sugar
    salad dressing   ¼ cup vinegar

Combine all ingredients and beat with rotary beater until thoroughly blended.

An excellent all-purpose dressing, especially good for slaw.

Harvest Slaw

(Ten servings)

1 cup salad dressing   2 tablespoons undiluted evaporated
1 teaspoon salt   milk
small dash of pepper   about 8 cups shredded cabbage
pinch of paprika   2 tablespoons grated onion
1 teaspoon sugar   ⅔ cup diced celery
2 tablespoons vinegar   ⅔ cup minced green pepper
    ⅔ cup grated raw carrot

Blend the salad dressing, salt, pepper, paprika, sugar, vinegar and milk and set aside. Combine cabbage and vegetables, tossing gently to mix. Cover the bowl and chill until just before serving. Shake dressing and pour over cabbage mixture. Stir gently with a fork, and serve.

One of the best recipes for a basic slaw. Much in favor for all kinds of suppers.

Goober Slaw

(Six servings)

5 to 6 cups finely chopped cabbage
1 large banana, peeled and diced
⅓ cup chopped salted peanuts

½ cup mayonnaise or salad dressing
¼ cup orange juice

Combine cabbage, banana and peanuts. Blend mayonnaise and orange juice well. Pour over cabbage and mix gently with a fork. Serve at once.

This most unusual salad is awfully good.

Basic Potato Salad

(Eight servings)

6 large potatoes, peeled
1½ tablespoons salad oil
1½ tablespoons vinegar
1 small onion, peeled and minced

4 hard-cooked eggs, shelled and
 chopped
about ¾ cup creamy salad dressing
salt and pepper to taste

Cook potatoes in boiling salted water until just tender. Drain, and break potatoes apart with a fork while still hot. Blend oil and vinegar and sprinkle over the potatoes. Cool, then add the onion and eggs. Mix with the dressing, using only enough to make the potatoes rather moist: the amount will depend on the size, etc., of the potatoes. Season to taste with salt and pepper. Chill well before serving.

This is my mother's rule and mine, in turn. I have found no reason to change it, for I consider it one of the best basic rules for this salad. Like my mother, I prefer salad dressing to mayonnaise for this. I never use cold boiled potatoes, but always boil them fresh when making salad. And I agree with her that old potatoes are to be preferred to new for potato salad.

Picnic Frolics

At the old-time church picnics there was always potato salad, although salads weren't in much favor with either men or children. If a lady brought a fancy affair garnished with plenty of garden lettuce, some man was sure to call out jovially, "Pass the ensilage, will you?" And another would answer, "Here 'tis. I ain't no rabbit!"

Milk cans of lemonade were a luscious treat, for at home no one dreamed of buying lemons to make cold drinks. (Switchel— a vinegar-molasses-ginger quencher—was the thrifty summer beverage on farms roundabouts.) As the lemonade was ladled out, small boys would chant: "Lemonade! Made in the shade! By an old maid!" I have since wondered if that particular bit of humor was as painful to the several spinsters at the picnic as it was hysterically funny to the small boys.

Lu's Caesar Salad

(Six servings)

1 egg	1 teaspoon Worcestershire sauce
¾ cup salad oil	¼ cup grated Parmesan cheese
¼ cup lemon juice	3 slices bread
1 teaspoon salt	1 clove garlic
½ teaspoon pepper	about 6 cups salad greens

Break the egg into simmering water for 1 minute. Remove, place in a bowl, and whip until fluffy with a rotary beater. Add oil gradually, beating constantly. Beat in the lemon juice, salt, pepper, Worcestershire sauce and cheese. Toast the bread, and, while it is still warm, rub each side of the slices with the garlic, cut in half. Cut toast slices in small cubes. Add to the salad greens, then toss gently with the egg and oil mixture. Serve at once.

A wonderfully flavored salad, and a great favorite with the menfolks.

Pennsylvania Dutch Lettuce

(Six servings)

2 tablespoons undiluted evaporated
    milk
2 tablespoons mayonnaise or salad
    dressing

3 tablespoons sugar
3 tablespoons vinegar
small pinch of salt
1 medium head of lettuce

Combine first five ingredients in small covered jar and shake vigorously until blended. Tear lettuce into attractive pieces. Pour dressing over lettuce and turn gently with a fork until all the leaves are coated with the dressing. Serve at once.

This is a rather sweet but delicious dressing for lettuce. It also makes an excellent dressing for slaw.

Orange-Onion Tossed Salad

(Four servings)

juice of ½ a small orange
1 tablespoon mayonnaise or salad
    dressing
2 teaspoons sugar
small pinch of salt

½ a medium head of lettuce
½ an orange, peeled and thinly
    sliced
2 tablespoons minced mild onion

Blend well together the orange juice, mayonnaise, sugar and salt. Tear lettuce into attractive chunks and place in a bowl. Cut each orange slice into quarters and add. Add onion. Pour orange juice mixture over all and toss gently to mix. Serve at once.

Out of the ordinary, and a very good salad indeed.

Old-fashioned Crock Salad

(Eight servings)

2 large tomatoes, unpeeled
2 large sweet green peppers, seeded
2 large mild onions, peeled
1½ cups vinegar

1½ cups salad oil
⅔ cup sugar
2 tablespoons salt
1 teaspoon celery seed

Slice vegetables very thin, separating onion slices into rings. Place all in large glass or enamelware bowl (in bygone years an earthenware crock was used, but few people have such a utensil now). Combine vinegar, oil, sugar, salt and celery seed. Mix well, then pour over the vetetables. Cover and let stand 24 hours. Stir once or twice during this period.

A favorite of other days and every bit as tasty today. It's really best as a side-dish.

Four-Bean Salad

(Eight to ten servings)

1 (1-lb.) can whole green beans, drained	2 medium onions, peeled
1 (1-lb.) can yellow wax beans, drained	1 medium green pepper, seeded
1 (1-lb.) can red kidney beans, drained	3 medium stalks celery, trimmed
1 can garbanzos (chick peas), drained	1 cup vinegar
	½ cup water
	1 cup sugar
	½ cup salad oil
	1 teaspoon salt

Put drained green and yellow beans in a saucepan, cover with fresh water. Simmer 5 minutes, then drain. Put drained kidney beans in a colander and rinse well with fresh water, then drain well. Combine vinegar, water and sugar and boil 2 minutes. Remove from heat and add oil and salt, mixing well. Combine beans in a large bowl. Cut onions, green pepper and celery in thin slices and add to beans. Pour the vinegar mixture over beans and mix in well. Cover and let stand in refrigerator several hours or overnight. The longer they stand, the better the flavor. Stir occasionally.

Something for Tomorrow

It was a pretty sure thing that the entire membership, except those actually ill enough to be housebound, would attend the ladies' society's regular meeting. The men declared slyly that no woman dared to miss a monthly session since the absent ones were apt to come under discussion.

There were seldom any programs. Members were expected to sew on articles for the next sale or bazaar. The Work Committee had previously cut out a supply of aprons, pot-holders or baby bibs. These were passed out, along with needles and thread.

As the meeting neared its end, knots were tied, threads snipped and articles neatly folded to be gathered up again. Years ago, one old lady, a spinster dressed always in rusty black silk, had a habit which fascinated me. As the time to gather the sewing approached, she anchored her needle firmly in the bosom of her black silk shirtwaist. At the same time she wound off a length of thread which she tucked into what she referred to as her "reticule."

No woman present would have dreamed of asking for the needle or the length of thread. Everyone knew Miss E——. As Father said, "Why shouldn't she have money laid up? She never spends any."

When sandwiches or cookies were passed, Miss E—— always took two of each variety. One she ate, the other she carefully wrapped in a paper napkin and stored with the thread in her reticule. It must have been sharply disappointing to her thrifty soul when some hostess elected to serve a fancy jellied salad or luscious dessert which could only be eaten with a spoon.

Tomato-Cheese Aspic Salad

(Four servings)

1½ cups tomato juice
1 tablespoon grated onion
1 teaspoon Worcestershire sauce
2 teaspoons lemon juice

3 drops Tabasco sauce
pinch of salt
1 (3-oz.) package lemon gelatine
¼ cup crumbled Blue cheese

Combine first six ingredients and bring just to boiling point. Add gelatine and stir until dissolved. Cool, then chill until partially thickened. Fold in crumbled blue cheese. Pour into 1-quart mold and chill until firm. Unmold on lettuce and serve with mayonnaise.

A piquant combination of flavors.

Jellied Tomato Salad

(Six servings)

1 (1-lb.) can stewed tomatoes (with green peppers and onion)
⅓ cup water
2 tablespoons vinegar
1 (3-oz.) package raspberry gelatine

Combine ½ cup of the liquid from the tomatoes with the water and the vinegar. Heat just to boiling point. Add gelatine and stir until dissolved. Add undrained can of tomatoes, breaking up the large chunks of tomato with a fork. Pour into a 1-quart mold or 6 individual ones. Chill until firm. Unmold on lettuce and serve with mayonnaise.

Molded Rhubarb Salad

(Five servings)

1½ cups diced rhubarb
¼ cup sugar
small pinch of salt
1 (3-oz.) package strawberry
gelatine
1 cup cold water
2 tablespoons lemon juice
1 cup diced celery

Combine rhubarb, sugar and salt. Place over very low heat. Cover and let come to boiling point. Don't stir or add any water. When rhubarb has simmered until tender, remove from heat and add gelatine. Stir until dissolved, then add cold water and lemon juice. Cool, then chill until it starts to thicken. Fold in celery. Pour into individual molds and chill until firm. Unmold on lettuce and garnish with mayonnaise.

Molded Cottage Cheese Fruit Salad

(Eight servings)

2 (3-oz.) packages mixed fruit-
    flavored gelatine
1¼ cups boiling water
2 tablespoons lemon juice

⅔ cup undiluted evaporated milk
2 tablespoons salad dressing
1 cup cottage cheese
1 (1-lb.) can fruit cocktail, undrained

Dissolve gelatine in the boiling water. Add lemon juice, evaporated milk, salad dressing and cottage cheese. Beat with rotary beater to blend all well. Add fruit cocktail. Pour into a 10 x 7 x 2 pan and chill until firm. Cut in squares and serve on lettuce. Garnish with mayonnaise or salad dressing.

Spring Salad

(Six servings)

1 (3-oz.) package lime gelatine
½ cup boiling water
1 undiluted can of cream of
    asparagus soup
1 tablespoon vinegar

2 teaspoons grated onion
½ cup mayonnaise or salad dressing
small pinch of pepper
1 cup minced cucumber

Dissolve gelatine in the boiling water. Add soup, vinegar, onion and mayonnaise. Stir until blended. Add pepper and cucumber. Pour into a 1-quart mold or 6 individual ones. Chill until firm. Unmold on lettuce and garnish with additional mayonnaise, if desired.

Cranberry Cream Molded Salad

(Six servings)

1 (3-oz.) package cherry gelatine
1 cup boiling water

1 cup whole-berry cranberry sauce
½ cup dairy soured cream

Dissolve gelatine in the boiling water, then stir in the cranberry sauce until blended. Add the soured cream, stirring hard until cream has blended thoroughly. Pour into a 1-quart mold and chill until firm. Unmold on lettuce and garnish with mayonnaise.

So simple, and so good with any poultry.

Molded Cranberry-Celery Salad

(Six servings)

1 envelope plain gelatine
1 cup cold water
1 (3-oz.) package cherry gelatine
1 cup boiling water
1 (1-lb.) can whole-berry cranberry

sauce
½ cup diced celery
3 tablespoons sweet pickle relish
2 tablespoons lemon juice

Soften plain gelatine in ½ cup of the cold water. Add, with the cherry gelatine, to the boiling water. Stir over low heat until all is dissolved. Add remaining ½ cup cold water. Add cranberry sauce and stir until well mixed. Add celery, relish and lemon juice. Pour into individual molds and chill until firm. Serve on lettuce with mayonnaise to garnish.

Spicy Peach and Orange Salad Mold

(Six to eight servings)

1 large (28-oz.) can sliced peaches
½ cup sugar
⅓ cup vinegar
large stick whole cinnamon

12 whole cloves
2 (3-oz.) packages orange gelatine
1¼ cups cold water

Drain peaches, reserving juice. Measure juice and add water to make 1½ cups liquid in all. Combine with the sugar, vinegar and spices. Bring to a boil and simmer 5 minutes. Add sliced peaches and simmer 5 minutes longer. Remove peaches and spices from syrup. Measure syrup and add boiling water to make 2½ cups in all. Dissolve the gelatine in this; add the cold water. Cool, then chill until it is the consistency of heavy syrup. Add the peaches and turn into a 10 x 6 glass cake pan. Chill until firm. Cut into squares and serve on lettuce, garnished with mayonnaise.

One of the best of all summer salads.

Jellied Cucumber-Lime Salad

(Six servings)

1 (3-oz.) package lime gelatine	¼ teaspoon salt
⅔ cup boiling water	1 cup dairy soured cream
¼ cup lemon juice	1 medium cucumber, peeled and
1 small onion, peeled and grated	grated

Dissolve the gelatine in the boiling water. Add lemon juice, grated onion and salt. Stir in soured cream and grated cucumber. Fill individual molds and chill until firm. Serve on lettuce garnished with mayonnaise.

A lovely tart salad, with a delicate green tint—especially good in hot weather.

Molded Pineapple and Cucumber Salad

(Six servings)

2 envelopes plain gelatine	¼ cup vinegar
¼ cup cold water	1 tablespoon lemon juice
1 cup boiling water	1 cup shredded cucumber
¼ cup sugar	1 cup crushed pineapple, undrained
½ teaspoon salt	

Soften the gelatine in the cold water for 5 minutes. Add boiling water and stir until gelatine has dissolved. Stir in sugar, salt, vinegar and lemon juice. Cool, then chill until mixture begins to thicken. Stir in cucumber and pineapple. Pour into 6 individual molds or a 1-quart one. Chill until firm. Unmold on lettuce and garnish with mayonnaise.

Down East Fish Hash

(Four servings)

1 small onion, peeled and diced	1 teaspoon salt
2 tablespoons melted fat	small pinch of pepper
2 cups diced cooked potatoes	1 teaspoon Worcestershire sauce
2 cups flaked cooked fish	⅔ cup undiluted evaporated milk
2 hard-cooked eggs, shelled and diced	

Simmer the onion in the melted fat for about 5 minutes. Add the potatoes, fish and eggs. Sprinkle with the salt and pepper. Add the Worcestershire sauce to the milk and stir into the fish-and-potato mixture. Cover and cook over moderate heat until hash is crusty and brown on the bottom. With pancake turner, turn the hash like an omelet and brown on other side. Serve piping hot.

An old-fashioned rule from the coast of Maine.

Meal Stops

Don't ever visit the South without tasting some of the wonderful native fish, both fresh- and salt-water varieties. Crisply fried catfish is second to none, and many restaurants feature it. Red snapper is without doubt one of the most delicious fish ever to be caught. Grouper and mullet, shad and bream, all rank high in quality.

Perhaps you'll be driving through a small south Florida town

and see a sign hung over the main street announcing "Church of God Fish Fry." Stop in for one of the best meals of your life—just as a sign saying "Ladies Benevolent Society Baked Bean Supper" means equally good food in Vermont.

Quick Seafood and Vegetable Pie

(Five to six servings)

1 (10-oz.) package frozen peas and carrots
1 undiluted can cream of mushroom soup
1 (7-oz.) can minced clams, undrained
1 (7-oz.) can tuna, undrained
½ teaspoon curry powder
1 batch Buttermilk Biscuits (*see* Breads)

Cook peas and carrots according to package directions. Drain. Add undrained clams to soup, then stir in undrained tuna. Stir until tuna is flaked. Add carrots and peas and the curry powder. Stir over low heat just until the boiling point is reached. Remove from heat and pour into a buttered 2-quart dish. Roll out biscuit dough and cut as usual. Arrange biscuits over top of fish and vegetable mixture. Bake in a 400 oven for about 25 minutes or until biscuits are crispy brown. Serve at once.

This good dish can be prepared and cooked in less than 45 minutes.

Salmon Loaf with Mushroom Sauce

(Six servings)

1 tall can salmon, undrained
2 cups soft breadcrumbs
⅓ cup sliced stuffed olives
1 cup grated cheese
½ cup chopped fresh parsley
1 cup milk
3 eggs, beaten
1 small onion, peeled and minced
¼ cup lemon juice
salt and pepper to taste

Remove bones and skin from undrained salmon. Flake the fish and combine with breadcrumbs, olives, cheese and parsley. Add 1 cup of milk to the beaten eggs, then stir in the onion. Add to salmon mixture, then add lemon juice. Add salt and pepper to taste, mixing well. Pour into a buttered 1½-quart casserole or standard size bread tin. Set in a larger pan of hot water and bake in a 350 oven for about 1 hour, or until knife blade comes out clean when inserted in center of loaf. Serve hot with a generous spoonful of Mushroom Sauce.

This is a firm, extremely good fish loaf.

Mushroom Sauce

(About 1½ cups)

1 undiluted can cream of mushroom
   soup

½ cup milk

Combine the can of soup with the ½ cup of milk, and heat just to boiling point. Serve hot over each portion of salmon loaf.

Salmon and Potato Salad

(Four to six servings)

1 (8-oz.) can salmon, drained and flaked	3 medium potatoes, cooked and diced
½ cup sliced stuffed olives	¼ cup dairy soured cream
½ cup diced cucumber	¼ cup mayonnaise or salad dressing
1 small onion, peeled and minced	1 teaspoon vinegar
	¼ teaspoon salt

Discard bones and skin from salmon. Combine fish with the olives, cucumber, onion and potato. Combine soured cream, mayonnaise, vinegar and salt. Blend well, then mix gently with potato mixture. Cover and chill. Serve on salad greens.

An extremely good main-dish salad.

Salmon Soufflé

(Six servings)

1 tall can salmon, undrained	4 eggs, separated
2 tablespoons melted butter or margarine	1/4 teaspoon thyme
	1/2 teaspoon curry powder
3 tablespoons flour	1/4 teaspoon salt
about 3/4 cup of milk	small pinch of pepper

Drain salmon, reserving the liquid; remove skin and bones and flake the fish. Blend the melted butter with the flour. To drained salmon liquid add enough milk to make 1 cup, blend into butter and flour and heat until smooth and thickened. Remove from heat. Beat egg yolks well, then beat in milk mixture very gradually. Add the seasonings and salmon, then fold in stiffly beaten egg whites. Pour into buttered 2-quart casserole and bake in a 350 oven for about 40 minutes, or until puffed high and browned. Serve at once.

Curry and thyme give a slightly different, very delicious flavor.

Scalloped Oysters

(Eight servings)

2 cups unsalted cracker crumbs	1 teaspoon salt
1 1/4 cups soft breadcrumbs	small dash of pepper
1 cup melted butter or margarine	1/2 cup oyster liquor
1 quart oysters	1/4 cup milk

Combine crumbs and melted butter. Make a layer of 1/3 of the crumbs in a buttered 2-quart casserole. Drain the oysters and reserve the liquor. Cover the crumb layer with 1/2 the oysters, sprinkle with 1/2 the salt and pepper. Combine 1/2 cup of the oyster liquor and the milk, pour 1/2 of this mixture over oyster layer. Repeat layers. Top with the remaining 1/3 of the crumbs. Bake in a 350 oven for about 50 minutes, or until the mixture is puffy and browned.

Native Tongue

I grew up understanding and loving the homely figures of speech of the Vermont hill-country; of late years, I've grown to understand and love the local figures of speech of the rural South.

At a Fish Fry one hot evening that ended a blistering hot day, I sat beside a Southern family. We exchanged comments on the weather, and the father, mopping energetically at his perspiring face and neck, observed, "Well, I tell you. Today has been a real toad-strangler." A little later on, his shy little wife told me the ages of her children. "I've only got one lap-baby now," she said. "The rest have all grown into yard-babies."

Jambalaya

(For eight)

1 cup uncooked rice
¼ cup melted fat
1 medium onion, thinly sliced
1 medium green pepper, seeded and diced
4 medium stalks celery, trimmed and diced
1 clove garlic, peeled and minced
1 cup diced cooked ham
pinch of thyme

3 drops Tabasco sauce
2 tablespoons flour
2 cups chicken broth
2 cups diced cooked chicken
2 (8-oz.) cans tomato sauce
1 cup cooked shrimp, or 1 (4-oz.) can, drained
⅔ cup fresh oysters or 1 (5-oz.) can, drained
salt and pepper to taste

Cook rice according to package directions and drain. Simmer melted fat, onion, green pepper, celery, garlic and ham until lightly browned. Add thyme, Tabasco and flour. Stir in chicken broth, chicken and tomato sauce. Add rice, and turn into a buttered 2-quart baking dish. Cover and bake in a 350 oven for 30 minutes. Remove, stir in shrimp and oysters. Taste and add salt and pepper as desired. Cook 15 minutes longer.

This tasty dish stands well and can be re-heated the next day if refrigerated well in the meantime.

Deviled Clams

(Four to six servings)

¼ cup + 2 tablespoons melted
    butter or margarine
¼ cup minced onion
¼ cup minced celery
1 clove garlic, peeled and minced
1 tablespoon flour
1 tablespoon catsup
½ teaspoon salt
pinch of pepper

¼ teaspoon thyme
3 drops Tabasco sauce
2 (7-oz.) cans minced clams,
    undrained
1 beaten egg
1 cup fine dry breadcrumbs
2 tablespoons chopped parsley
paprika

Simmer ¼ cup butter, the onion, celery and garlic for about 5 minutes. Stir in flour and catsup, then add the seasonings. Add clams and bring just to boiling point. Add ½ cup of the crumbs, the parsley and the beaten egg. Bring to boiling point again, then pour into a buttered 1½-quart baking dish. Combine the remaining 2 tablespoons melted butter with the remaining ½ cup crumbs, scatter over the top of the clam mixture, and dust with paprika. Bake about 15 minutes in a 425 oven or until golden brown and bubbling hot. Serve at once.

Clam Pie

(Six servings)

2 (7-oz.) cans minced clams
¾ cup milk
2 eggs, beaten
½ cup unsalted cracker crumbs

1 teaspoon seasoned salt
small pinch of pepper
2 tablespoons butter or margarine
Pie Pastry for 2 crusts (*see* Pies)

Drain clams, reserving ¾ cup of the liquid. Combine liquid with the milk and beaten eggs. Stir in cracker crumbs, clams, salt and pepper. Mix well, then pour into pastry-lined pie tin. Dot with the butter, then cover with the top crust, well slitted. Bake 10 minutes in a 450 oven. Reduce heat to 350 and bake about 30 minutes longer.

The filling is custardy and well flavored with the clams.

Maybe It Was Confucius

In Eatonville, Florida, near Orlando, there is a beautiful little church of historic significance, and with unusual wall paintings, that is being repaired by the efforts of its all-black congregation. Determined to raise the necessary money without asking for donations from anyone, the members have put into effect a long-range plan: On weekends, the women cook either fried-fish or chicken dinners, which the men deliver to anyone who orders them, the price being around a dollar.

It calls to mind those days not so long ago when miles of cakes, pies, doughnuts and bread were sold at food sales, while plays, suppers and dances went on continually to help swell the Thetford (Vermont) Academy building fund.

Someone told me once of an ancient Chinese saying: "The longest journey starts with the first step."

Baked Fillet of Sole with Shrimp Sauce

(Four servings)

1 pound fillets of sole (or flounder)	2 tablespoons cracker crumbs
½ teaspoon seasoned salt	1 tablespoon melted butter or
1 can frozen cream of shrimp soup,	margarine
undiluted	pinch of paprika
½ cup milk	

Arrange fish in a buttered 6 x 10 baking dish. Sprinkle with the seasoned salt. Combine thawed soup with the milk and stir until smooth. Pour over fish. Combine crumbs and melted butter and scatter over fish and sauce. Sprinkle with paprika. Cover and bake in a 400 oven for 10 minutes. Uncover and bake 10 to 15 minutes longer, or until brown and bubbling hot. Serve at once.

Curried Shrimp and Eggs

(Six servings)

2 cans cream of mushroom soup, undiluted	4 hard-cooked eggs, shelled and sliced
1 cup light cream	2 cups cooked shrimps
2 teaspoons curry powder	about 3 cups cooked rice

Combine soup, cream and curry powder. Stir over low heat until just at boiling point, but don't allow mixture to boil. Add eggs and shrimps. Heat all very hot and serve at once spooned over hot rice.

Individual Shrimp Casseroles

(For four)

¼ pound butter or margarine	¼ cup sifted flour
¼ cup minced onion	½ teaspoon dry mustard
1 pound raw shrimps, shelled and de-veined	1 (4-oz.) can mushrooms, sliced
1 teaspoon salt	1 tall can evaporated milk, undiluted
pinch of pepper	water
	¼ cup grated Parmesan cheese

Melt butter in a frying pan, add onion and shrimp and stir over low heat until the shrimp are pink and the onion is tender, about 10 minutes. Add salt and pepper. Combine flour and mustard and stir into the shrimps. Drain mushrooms, reserving liquid. Measure liquid and add enough water to make ⅔ cup in all. Combine with evaporated milk, add to the shrimp mixture and stir over low heat until thickened. Add the mushrooms. Pour into 4 buttered individual casseroles. Sprinkle Parmesan cheese over the tops and bake in a 350 oven until bubbling hot and browned, about 20 minutes. Serve hot with toast points.

Shrimp Rarebit

(Four servings)

1 can cream of tomato soup, undiluted	small dash of pepper
1 cup shredded sharp cheese (¼ lb.)	1 pound small shrimp, cooked, shelled and de-veined
1 teaspoon Worcestershire sauce	1 cup dairy soured cream
½ teaspoon salt	1 tablespoon butter or margarine

Combine first five ingredients and place over low heat. Cook, stirring constantly, until cheese has melted. Add the shrimp (if shrimp are not small, cut each in two or three pieces); stir over low heat until shrimp are heated through. Stir in soured cream and the butter. Continue stirring over low heat until just at boiling point but don't allow mixture to boil. Serve hot over crackers or hot toast points.

Crabmeat Casserole

(Four to five servings)

1 (7-oz.) can crabmeat	6 hard-cooked eggs
1 cup dry poultry stuffing mix	1 cup cooked green peas
1 cup milk	1 tablespoon melted butter or margarine
1 cup creamy salad dressing	
1 tablespoon minced parsley	3 tablespoons dry breadcrumbs
1 tablespoon minced onion	

Pick crabmeat into flakes, discarding tendons, and add stuffing mix, milk, salad dressing, parsley and onion, mixing lightly. Shell and slice the eggs and fold them into the crabmeat mixture; fold in the peas. Turn into a greased casserole. Combine melted butter and breadcrumbs, sprinkle over the top and bake in a 375 oven for about 35 minutes, or until top is browned and all is bubbling hot.

This is a treasure—quick, easy and good.

Tuna Cups with Mustard Sauce

(Six servings)

2 (7-oz.) cans tuna, drained and
    flaked
2 eggs, slightly beaten
½ cup milk
¼ cup catsup
1 tablespoon melted butter or

margarine
1 cup quick-cooking oats
½ teaspoon salt
¼ teaspoon pepper
3 tablespoons chopped celery
¼ cup minced onion

Combine tuna and slightly beaten eggs. Stir in milk, catsup and melted butter. Add oats, salt, pepper, celery and onion. Mix all well, then pour into 12 standard-size buttered muffin cups, filling about ¾ full. Top with the Mustard Sauce. Bake in a 350 oven for about 45 minutes. Serve hot.

This is an unusual recipe, and unusually good.

MUSTARD SAUCE

(One generous cup)

1½ tablespoons melted butter
    or margarine
1 tablespoon flour
1 teaspoon prepared mustard

1 cup chicken broth
½ teaspoon bottled horseradish
¼ teaspoon salt
small pinch of pepper

Blend butter and flour; add mustard, then blend in chicken broth. Stir over low heat until smooth and thickened. Remove from heat, add horseradish, salt and pepper.

Good Baked Tuna Roll

(Six servings)

2 cups sifted flour
1 teaspoon salt
4 teaspoons baking powder
¼ cup softened shortening
1 beaten egg
¾ cup milk

1 (7-oz.) can tuna, drained and
  flaked
2 teaspoons grated onion
1½ tablespoons chopped fresh
  parsley
¼ cup sweet pickle relish

Sift flour with ½ teaspoon of the salt and the baking powder. Rub in shortening. Add ½ cup of the milk and the beaten egg, mixing just enough to wet all ingredients. Knead slightly on floured board and roll out to about ¼ inch thick. Combine tuna, parsley, onion, the remaining ½ teaspoon salt and the remaining ¼ cup milk; add the relish, mixing well. Spread mixture over the sheet of dough, then roll as for jelly roll. Place on a greased pan and bake at 400 for about 40 minutes. Serve hot, sliced with Cheese Sauce spooned over each serving.

CHEESE SAUCE

(Nearly two cups)

3 tablespoons soft butter or
  margarine
2 tablespoons flour

1½ cups milk
½ cup shredded sharp cheese (2 oz.)

Blend butter and flour, add milk and stir over low heat until smooth and thick. Add shredded cheese, stir until melted and then remove from heat. Serve hot.

In Lieu of Cash

Many years ago the reception for a new minister often took the form of a Donation Party. Did those long-ago preachers and their wives mind receiving squares of salt pork, bags of potatoes, pounds of butter—whatever the donors had the most of at home?

In those days of little refrigeration, it would have been impossible to keep that much food unspoiled until eaten. It was the general belief that the minister hitched up his top buggy the day after the party and carried a portion of the load to a neighboring town, where he exchanged it for things the family needed more.

I used to wonder why people didn't trade in their donations first, and present the minister with that most welcome gift of all, the cash thereby derived. But Mother just said, "Folks wouldn't do it. This is the way it's always been done."

Tuna Macaroni Salad

(Eight servings)

½ pound elbow macaroni, cooked
    and drained
½ cup dairy soured cream
about ⅔ cup mayonnaise or salad
    dressing
¼ cup minced onion
¾ cup finely chopped celery

2 cups green peas, cooked
1 (7-oz.) can tuna fish, drained and
    flaked
2 tablespoons lemon juice
¼ cup chopped stuffed olives
1 teaspoon salt
small pinch of pepper

Cool the cooked and drained macaroni, then add soured cream and mayonnaise, stirring gently to mix. Add onion, celery and green peas. Combine tuna and lemon juice, then add to first mixture. Add olives, then salt and pepper. Taste and add a bit more salt, if necessary. If the salad seems too dry for your taste, add a little more mayonnaise. Cover and chill until serving time. Serve on lettuce with any desired dressing as garnish.

A most attractive main dish.

Absent Cook's Stew

(For six)

2 pounds stewing beef, cubed	1 (10½-oz.) can condensed tomato
3 medium carrots, peeled and sliced	soup
2 medium onions, peeled and sliced	½ a soup can of water
3 medium potatoes, peeled and	2 tablespoons vinegar
quartered	1 teaspoon salt
1 small yellow turnip, peeled and	pinch of pepper
cubed (optional)	1 bay leaf

You will need for this a heavy casserole with closely fitting cover. Place the meat cubes in a casserole and arrange the vegetables around and through the cubes. Combine the remaining ingredients and pour over meat and vegetables. Cover and bake in a 275 oven for about 5 hours.

There is no need to watch this stew. The meat will be brown and succulent and the gravy richly flavored.

Pa's Favorite

When Joe P—— died, the women hustled into their kitchens to prepare tangible expressions of their respect and affection for the family. Having in her icebox the remnants of a New England boiled dinner, one neighbor prepared Red Flannel hash, well known to be a favorite dish in the P—— household. The widow took the towel-covered pan with appropriate words of gratitude, lifting a corner to glimpse the contents, and, smiling through tears, said: "Poor Pa—his favorite supper. And to think he ain't able to enjoy it."

Deviled Swiss Steak

(Six servings)

1½-pound slice of top-of-the-round steak	2 tablespoons melted fat
¼ cup flour	2 medium onions, peeled and sliced
2 teaspoons dry mustard	2 cups undrained canned tomatoes
1 teaspoon salt	1 tablespoon Worcestershire sauce
¼ teaspoon pepper	2 teaspoons brown sugar

Combine flour, mustard, salt and pepper, and rub the mixture well into the slice of steak so that every bit clings to the meat. Brown in the melted fat. Remove meat to a baking pan and arrange onion slices over the top. Pour tomatoes into the frying pan, stir in the Worcestershire sauce and brown sugar, then pour over the meat and onions. Cover and bake in a 350 oven for 1½ hours, or until the meat is tender. Serve with sauce from the pan spooned over each portion.

A rich brown sauce with a wonderful flavor.

New England Boiled Dinner

(For ten)

4 pounds corned beef	1 large cabbage, quartered
1 pound salt pork (optional)	8 large potatoes, peeled
1 large yellow turnip, peeled and cut up	8 parsnips, peeled (optional)
10 large carrots, peeled	12 small beets, unpeeled

Place corned beef and salt pork in a large kettle, cover with unsalted boiling water. Put on the lid and bring to a boil; skim after 10 minutes. Reduce heat and simmer for about 2½ hours, or until the corned beef is nearly tender, and add the cut-up turnip and the whole carrots. Place the washed beets in a saucepan and cover with salted water; cover and cook until tender, about 1 hour. After the turnip and carrots have cooked for about 30 minutes, add the cabbage and potatoes. If parsnips are used, add at this time. Cover and simmer until potatoes are tender, about 45 minutes. The corned beef should be very tender. Remove the meat to a large platter, drain the vegetables and arrange them around the meat, the beets in small mounds at either end of platter. Slice the meat to serve.

Rules for boiled dinners are many and vary according to locality and individual tastes. This is the way the ladies cooked them for Harvest Suppers when I served on the committee.

Traditional Red Flannel Hash

(For eight)

4 cups leftover corned beef	other leftover vegetables
4 cups cooked potatoes	salt to taste
4 cups cooked beets	fat for browning

This is usually made from whatever is left from a New England Boiled Dinner. The amounts given here are only intended as a guide. Some people insist that it should be made of only beets and potatoes added to the meat; others have their pet rules. In the Vermont hill-country we like it with enough beets to give the mixture a deep ruby red color.

Put the meat and vegetables through the food grinder, using a coarse knife. Mix lightly but well and salt to taste. Brown in the melted fat, using a large and heavy frying pan—an iron spider is ideal.

Hamburger and Onion Shortcake

(Four hearty servings)

1 tablespoon melted butter or
    margarine
4 medium onions, sliced thin
½ pound lean hamburger
1 teaspoon salt

¼ teaspoon pepper
2 eggs, beaten
1 cup dairy soured cream
paprika

Simmer butter and onions over low heat for about 10 minutes until tender but not brown. Add hamburger, stirring with a fork to crumble, and cook for about 5 minutes, or until meat loses its red color. Beat eggs, soured cream and seasonings well, and combine with meat mixture. Pour it over Biscuit Pastry, sprinkle with paprika, and bake in a 375 oven for about 35 minutes. Serve hot, cut in wedges.

A wonderful recipe—old-fashioned zestiness for hungry people!

BISCUIT PASTRY

(Nine-inch pan)

1 cup sifted flour
½ teaspoon salt
1 teaspoon baking powder

½ teaspoon baking soda
2 tablespoons shortening
about ⅔ cup buttermilk

Sift flour with the salt, baking powder and soda. Rub in shortening, then mix with buttermilk to make a rather soft dough. Knead slightly on a floured board, then roll out to fit a lightly greased 9-inch pie tin. Press the dough in lightly, pour in filling, and bake as directed above.

Insurance Policy

Years ago, the cooking ability—good, bad or indifferent—of every woman for miles around was known to all. Threshing crews and corn-cutting gangs helped to spread the word.

Grandfather liked to tell about a certain deacon's household in which the cooking was notoriously poor. After an especially bad meal one year, one man in the threshing crew commented feelingly on the culinary abilities of the deacon's wife. "Well, I ain't saying she's a darned poor cook," he said. "But after eating that dinner just now, I can sure understand why her family says a few words to the Lord before they sit down to eat!"

Meatballs with Buttermilk Gravy

(Six servings)

1 pound hamburger
¼ cup soft breadcrumbs
½ cup milk
1 teaspoon salt

pinch of pepper
1 small onion, peeled and minced
1 beaten egg
3 tablespoons melted fat

Combine hamburger, crumbs, salt, pepper, onion and beaten egg, mixing well. Form into 12 medium-sized balls and brown in the melted fat. Remove balls from the skillet as they brown (reserve the fat), then add them all carefully to the Buttermilk Gravy. Cover the pan and leave over very low heat about ½ hour, for the meatballs to cook through and for the flavors to blend, stirring gently from time to time to prevent sticking-on. Serve 2 meatballs per person.

The buttermilk adds a fine touch to the gravy.

BUTTERMILK GRAVY

(About 2 cups)

reserved fat
¼ cup flour
¼ teaspoon salt
small dash of pepper

2 teaspoons sugar
1 teaspoon dry mustard
2 cups buttermilk
1 small egg, beaten

Stir the flour into the fat left in the skillet after meatballs are browned, then add salt, pepper, sugar and mustard. Stir in the buttermilk and beaten egg. Continue cooking over low heat until the gravy reaches the boiling point, stirring to prevent sticking or lumping. Add the browned meatballs, and continue cooking as described above.

Stuffed Meatballs

(Six servings)

½ pound ground beef
½ pound ground pork
½ pound ground veal
2 slices dry bread, rolled into crumbs
1 egg, slightly beaten
1 teaspoon salt
¼ teaspoon pepper
1 medium onion, peeled and minced

12 firm cooked prunes
12 stuffed olives
melted fat for browning
1 can cream of mushroom soup,
    undiluted
⅔ cup undiluted evaporated milk
3 cups cooked rice or noodles

Combine meats, add the crumbs and mix in the beaten egg, salt, pepper and onion. Combine well, then form into 24 thin patties. Remove the pit from each prune and replace with a stuffed olive. Place a prune on a patty, cover with another patty and form into a large ball. Dust each ball with a little flour and brown lightly in a little melted fat. Remove balls to a heavy skillet. Pour soup and milk into the frying pan. Stir until well blended. Pour over meatballs. Cover and simmer over very low heat for about 30 minutes. Serve 2 per person with hot rice or noodles.

Hamburger Stroganoff

(Four to six servings)

¼ cup butter or margarine
1 medium onion, peeled and minced
1 pound lean hamburger
2 tablespoons flour
½ teaspoon salt
pinch of pepper

1 can cream of chicken soup,
    undiluted
1 (4-oz.) can mushrooms, drained
1 cup dairy soured cream
2½ to 3 cups cooked rice

Simmer butter and onion for 5 minutes; add hamburger and stir until meat is lightly browned. Sprinkle the flour over the meat and stir to mix, add salt and pepper, and stir in the soup and mushrooms. Cover and simmer 15 minutes. Add soured cream. Heat very hot but *do not boil.* Serve at once with hot boiled rice. Or noodles.

Quick and Easy Beef Noodles

(Four to six servings)

1 tablespoon melted fat	1 (1 lb.-2 oz.) can tomato juice
2 medium onions, peeled and diced	2 teaspoons Worcestershire sauce
1 clove garlic, peeled and minced	½ teaspoon salt
⅔ pound lean hamburger	½ teaspoon celery salt
½ pound uncooked medium-wide	small pinch of pepper
noodles	½ cup dairy soured cream

Simmer melted fat, onions and garlic for about 10 minutes, then add the hamburger. Stir with a fork to separate the meat, and cook until red color disappears. Spread the uncooked noodles over the surface of the meat. Combine tomato juice, Worcestershire sauce, salt, celery salt and pepper, pour over the noodles. Cover and simmer over very low heat for about 30 minutes. Stir in the soured cream, heat just below boiling point. Serve at once.

"Pass the Gravy"

When the gravy supply appears to be inadequate, it may be extended in several ingenious ways. Bouillon cubes, meat sauces, gravy coloring and flavoring products can all be utilized. It is, however, desirable to have at least a few spoonfuls of pan drippings for basic flavor.

A quart of excellent meat gravy may be made by blending 4 tablespoons of pan drippings, 4 tablespoons of flour and 2 tea-

spoons of Worcestershire sauce, then blending in 1 quart of water and stirring over low heat until smooth and thickened.

Another simple gravy may be made by draining a 4-ounce can of sliced mushrooms, reserving the liquid. Sauté the mushrooms in 4 tablespoons of melted butter or pan drippings. Blend in 4 tablespoons of flour, then add the mushroom liquid combined with 3 cups of water and 3 bouillon cubes. Stir and boil for 1 minute.

When leftover meats or poultry to be used lack accompanying gravy, simmer available bones in water just barely covering. Thicken and season the broth to taste, then add gravy coloring.

Southwest Meat Pie

(Six servings)

4 large slices bacon	small pinch of pepper
1 pound hamburger	1 (8-oz.) can tomato sauce
1 cup drained whole-kernel corn	1 egg
¼ cup finely chopped green pepper	¼ cup milk
1 small onion, finely chopped	½ teaspoon dry mustard
¼ cup cornmeal	½ teaspoon Worcestershire sauce
½ teaspoon oregano	1 cup shredded sharp cheese (¼ lb.)
½ teaspoon chili powder	6 stuffed olives, sliced
1 teaspoon salt	unbaked 9-inch Pie Shell (*see* Pies)

Fry bacon until crisp, drain. Pour off the fat, then brown hamburger in the pan. Add vegetables, cornmeal, oregano, chili powder, salt, pepper and tomato sauce. Stir all well, pour mixture into the Pie Shell. Bake in a 425 oven for 25 minutes; remove. Beat together the egg and milk, mustard and Worcestershire sauce, and stir in the cheese. Spread over the top of the pie, then scatter sliced olives over all. Crumble the bacon and scatter over olives. Return pie to the oven and bake 15 minutes longer, or until cheese has melted. Remove from the oven and let stand 10 minutes before serving.

This excellent main-dish pie is not overly spicy.

Favorite Chili Con Carne

(Six servings)

3 tablespoons melted fat	1 (8-oz.) can tomato sauce
1 medium onion, peeled and diced	1 tablespoon chili powder
1 small clove of garlic, peeled and minced	1 teaspoon salt
	1 teaspoon Worcestershire sauce
1 pound lean hamburger	2 (1-lb.) cans red kidney beans

Simmer melted fat, onion and garlic together for about 5 minutes. Add hamburger and cook until red color has gone, breaking the meat apart with a fork. Add remaining ingredients and cook, covered, over very low heat for about 1 hour.

This is the chili recipe I like best. It's not too hot for the average taste. More chili powder can be added if you like it hotter.

Baked Corned Beef Hash

(For four)

1 tablespoon melted fat	1 (12-oz.) can corned beef, coarsely chopped
1 small onion, peeled and diced	
2 tablespoons catsup	2 cups seasoned mashed potatoes
2 tablespoons dairy soured cream	2 tablespoons grated sharp cheese

Simmer fat and onion together for 5 minutes. Add catsup, soured cream and corned beef. Combine well, then add mashed potato. Mix gently and turn into a greased 1½-quart baking dish. Sprinkle the cheese over the top and bake in a 375 oven for about 50 minutes.

Creamed cabbage goes beautifully with this good old-fashioned dish.

Baked Liver Loaf

(For six to eight)

1½ pounds beef liver, cut in strips
½ cup dry breadcrumbs
1 medium onion, peeled
¾ pound bulk sausage meat
1 teaspoon salt
¼ teaspoon pepper

pinch each of marjoram, rosemary
   and basil
¼ teaspoon poultry seasoning
1 egg, slightly beaten
⅓ cup undiluted evaporated milk
4 large strips of bacon, cut in half

Dredge liver strips in the crumbs, and put them through your food grinder, using the medium knife. Put the onion through the grinder, combine liver, onion and sausage meat. Mix in salt, pepper and herbs. Combine the egg and the milk and mix in, working thoroughly together. Pack the meat firmly into a greased, standard-size bread tin. Lay the half-strips of bacon over the top and bake in a 375 oven for about 1 hour. Serve hot or cold.

At our house we like this cold, like a pâté (which it resembles), with potato salad.

Pot Haggis

(For six)

1 pound beef liver
1½ cups boiling water
2 beef bouillon cubes
½ pound bulk sausage meat

1 large onion
1¼ cups quick oatmeal
¼ teaspoon salt
dash of cayenne pepper

Put liver, boiling water and bouillon cubes over moderate heat and simmer for about 15 minutes. Drain, reserving broth. Cool liver slightly, trim and put through the food grinder, using the coarse knife. Follow with the sausage, then the peeled onion. Combine with the oatmeal, salt and pepper, then add the reserved broth. Mix well, then turn into buttered 1½-quart heavy bowl. Cover tightly with foil. Place on a rack in a deep kettle and pour in hot water up to half the height of the bowl. Cover the kettle and simmer about 2 hours. Serve hot.

This is a flavorful variation of an old-time Scottish dish.

Turkish Lamb Pilaf

(Six servings)

1½ pounds lean lamb, cubed
2 tablespoons melted fat
1 large onion, peeled and diced
1½ cups uncooked rice
½ teaspoon ground allspice
1 teaspoon salt

dash of pepper
3 cups boiling water
2 chicken bouillon cubes
½ pound uncooked prunes,
  plumped in boiling water

Brown lamb cubes in the melted fat. Remove meat; add onion, cover and cook gently until onion is tender but not browned. Add rice, seasonings, boiling water and bouillon cubes, stirring until cubes have dissolved. Pit and quarter each prune, add to meat-rice mixture. Turn into a buttered 2-quart baking dish, cover and bake about 1 hour, or until meat is very tender. Serve hot.

Baked Lamb Shanks with Curried Rice

(Four servings)

4 lamb shanks
meat tenderizer
1 teaspoon seasoned salt
2 teaspoons curry powder
¼ teaspoon ground ginger

1 medium onion, peeled and diced
1 medium apple, peeled and diced
2 cups hot water
1 cup uncooked rice
1 tablespoon lemon juice

Pierce lamb shanks several times with a sharp fork, sprinkle on tenderizer according to bottle directions. Place meat in a baking dish and bake uncovered in a 450 oven until browned, about 30 minutes. Combine salt, curry powder and ginger, and sprinkle the mixture on the meat. Add diced onion and apple, then pour in the hot water. Cover and continue baking for 1 hour more at 400. Remove from oven, add lemon juice and rice, mixing with pan liquid; cover and return to oven. Bake about 45 minutes longer, or until meat is very tender. If rice looks dry, add a little more hot water.

Pork and Vegetables, Chinese Style
(Four to six servings)

2 tablespoons vegetable oil	½ teaspoon salt
⅔ cup instant rice	1½ cups boiling water
1 large onion, thinly sliced	1 beef bouillon cube
4 large stalks celery	1 tablespoon soy sauce
1 large green pepper	1 can luncheon meat (12-oz.)

Simmer oil, rice and onion until lightly browned. Cut celery in thin diagonal slices, and green pepper in strips; add to rice with salt, boiling water and bouillon cube. Cover and simmer 10 minutes, stirring occasionally. Add soy sauce. Cut luncheon meat in thin strips and add. Cover and simmer 10 minutes longer, or until vegetables are just barely tender: they should be slightly crisp.

Tasty, quick and inexpensive.

Hand Across the Years

In spite of his great age, old Gideon B—— usually attended all the suppers, his shaggy white head in a place of honor at one end of a long table. The children hung around him, for he was full of marvelous tales of things when the town was young. And always, before the evening was over, he'd hold out a knobby old hand to first one child, then another, saying, "Shake the hand that many times touched the hand of a man that shook hands with George Washington."

I rather doubted him, because the great general seemed to me to be lost in the mists of years. But Father explained it to us. "You see, Gideon is 'way over ninety right now. He was born in 1820, right here in Thetford. And his grandfather, the one that was with George Washington in the Revolution, didn't die until about 1830. So Gideon remembers all about him and, of course, must have held his grandfather's hand many times."

It made George Washington very close, almost as if he had lived up on our mountain road, too.

Orange-glazed Pork Chops

(For four)

4 large pork chops
salt, pepper and flour
1 tablespoon melted fat
½ cup orange juice

2 tablespoons orange marmalade
2 tablespoons brown sugar
1 tablespoon vinegar

Dust chops lightly with salt and pepper, then dredge lightly in flour. Brown on both sides in the melted fat. Combine orange juice, marmalade, sugar and vinegar, and pour evenly over the chops. Cover the pan and simmer for about 45 minutes, or until meat is very tender. Remove pan cover during the last 10 minutes of cooking time. Serve sauce spooned over each chop.

An excellent variation for pork chops.

Baked Barbecued Pork Chops

(For four)

4 thick (1-in.) pork chops
3 tablespoons catsup
1½ tablespoons lemon juice
2 teaspoons Worcestershire sauce
1 tablespoon grated onion

¼ teaspoon dry mustard
½ teaspoon salt
¼ teaspoon paprika
pinch of curry powder
½ cup hot water

Place chops in a heavy baking dish. Blend remaining ingredients together, pour over the chops. Cover and bake for 30 minutes in a 350 oven. Turn chops and bake 30 minutes longer, or until meat is tender and browned. If chops do not seem to be browning sufficiently, remove the cover the last 10 minutes of baking time.

Piquant barbecue flavor, not too spicy.

Roast Loin of Pork Oriental

(For six)

loin of pork (*c.* 5 lbs.)	¼ teaspoon pepper
2 teaspoons grated orange rind	¼ teaspoon thyme
2 teaspoons seasoned salt	¼ cup orange juice
½ teaspoon ground ginger	2 tablespoons honey
½ teaspoon dry mustard	

Rub the pork well with a mixture of the orange rind, salt, ginger, mustard, pepper and thyme. Roast in a 350 oven for 2½ to 3 hours, or until meat is quite tender. During the last 15 minutes of cooking, mix the orange juice and honey well and pour over the meat. When the meat thermometer registers 185°, remove the meat to a serving platter. Pour off any excess fat, and thicken the pan liquid with flour paste to make the gravy.

The meat will be brown and crusty, with a deliciously spicy flavor.

Baked Ham with Pineapple Glaze

(For twenty)

1 tenderized ham (*c.* 10 lbs.)	whole cloves
about 2 tablespoons prepared mustard	¾ cup light brown sugar
	⅓ cup undrained crushed pineapple

Place the ham fat side up on a rack in the roasting pan. Bake in a 325 oven for about 2½ hours—if you use a meat thermometer, the internal heat should reach 160. Take the ham from the oven and turn the heat up to 450. Meanwhile, remove the rind carefully and cut the fatty layer in a diamond pattern, being careful not to cut down into the meat. Brush mustard lightly over the ham and place a clove in the center of each diamond. Mix the brown sugar and pineapple and spread over the surface of the ham. Return it to the oven and bake 20 minutes, until the pine-

apple glaze is brown and crusty. Remove the ham from the oven and let it stand 20 minutes for easier slicing.

This is the favorite way of baking ham in my community. The glaze is one that everyone likes.

French Pork Pie

(Four to six servings)

2½ cups ground cooked pork
1 medium cold boiled potato
1 small onion, peeled
2 drops Tabasco sauce

1 tablespoon catsup
about 1¼ cups leftover pork gravy
salt and pepper to taste
Pie Pastry for 2 crusts

After grinding pork, put potato and onion through the grinder. Combine pork, potato, onion, Tabasco, catsup and ¼ cup of the gravy. Taste and add salt and pepper to suit individual taste. Mix well, pour into a pastry-lined pie tin. Cover with the top crust, sealing edges and slitting the center of the top. Bake in a 400 oven for 45 minutes. Serve with remaining hot gravy spooned over each wedge.

Sugar Maple

The minister's wife always lent a hand in fund-raising activities of the Society. The minister, too, puttered around trying to help—although most of the women whispered to each other that they'd be thankful if he'd just get out from under their feet! The Reverend and Mrs. W—— were very old when they were with us, two of the most remarkable people we had ever had in the parsonage. They were devoted to each other, and I remember him saying to his wife one day as she ruefully mentioned how white her hair was getting and how wrinkled her face, "You're like a maple tree, dear. In the spring you gave your sweetness. Now it's autumn. Remember that the maple is most beautiful then."

Sausage and Sweet Potatoes

(Four good servings)

1 (8-oz.) package brown-and-serve
    sausage links
1 (3-oz.) package orange gelatine
½ cup boiling water
¼ cup light brown sugar
2 tablespoons butter or margarine
1 teaspoon dry minced onion
1 teaspoon dry mustard

juice of 1 lemon
¼ teaspoon salt
pinch of pepper
1 (20-oz.) can sweet potatoes,
    drained
1 (20-oz.) can pineapple chunks,
    drained

Brown sausages according to package directions and remove from the pan. Combine gelatine and boiling water, pour into the pan, and add brown sugar, butter, onion, mustard, lemon juice, salt and pepper. Stir over moderate heat until the mixture boils. Add drained sweet potatoes and pineapple, reduce heat and simmer gently about 15 minutes. Add sausages and simmer 5 minutes longer. Serve at once.

This is an absolute gem of a rule. The orange flavor is very distinct.

Sausages and Green Peppers

(For six)

2 pounds link sausages
10 sweet green peppers (medium)
2 medium onions
pinch of thyme

pinch of sage
pinch of oregano
grated Parmesan cheese (optional)

Place sausages—do not prick them yet—in a heavy kettle and just barely cover with water; boil 15 minutes, then drain off and discard the water. Now, prick each sausage several times with a fork, allowing the fat to spurt into the kettle. Seed each pepper and cut in quarters. Peel onions and cut into chunks. Arrange peppers and onions over the top of the sausages. Add the seasonings. Cover the kettle and set over a very low flame, just hot enough to keep the contents simmering. Stir occasionally and add a tiny bit of hot water if the mixture cooks dry. Cook about 45 minutes. Serve at once with the grated Parmesan sprinkled over each portion, if desired. (I like it without.)

An utterly wonderful concoction. Hunks of warm Italian bread go beautifully with this. Sweet Italian sausages can be used instead of the regular variety.

Tolerance

It used to be that no supper ever began until the minister or one of the deacons said a lengthy grace. One night, the B——s had a new hired man with them. When everyone was seated, and without waiting an instant, the new man half rose in his chair and began spearing meat and potatoes to fill up his plate.

The minister held up his hand. "You'd better wait a minute," he said. "We always say something here before we eat."

The hired man went right on filling his plate. "Go right ahead," he said heartily, "say anything you durn please. You can't turn my stummick."

Rice Stuffing

(For 5-pound bird)

2 cups cold cooked rice
1 cup coarse dry breadcrumbs
1 teaspoon poultry seasoning
½ teaspoon salt
pinch of pepper

1 small onion, diced
2 tablespoons melted fat
1 medium stalk celery, diced
about ½ cup chicken broth, milk
    or water

Combine rice, breadcrumbs, poultry seasoning, salt and pepper. Cook onion and melted fat for 5 minutes; add celery and cook 5 minutes longer. Combine with the rice mixture, and moisten well with the broth. Toss gently with a fork, mixing thoroughly.

An extremely good stuffing and popular in the South.

A Good Chicken Barbecue Sauce

(About 2½ cups)

1 cup catsup
½ cup water
¼ cup lemon juice
1 small onion, peeled and chopped
1 small clove of garlic, minced

1 teaspoon salt
¼ teaspoon pepper
1 teaspoon paprika
1 tablespoon light brown sugar
2 tablespoons vegetable oil

Combine all ingredients except the oil. Simmer for 15 minutes. Remove from heat and add oil. Enough for 2 good-sized broilers.

In a closed jar, this sauce keeps very well in the refrigerator.

Paper-Bag Barbecued Chicken

(Four servings)

¼ cup melted vegetable shortening   1 cup any barbecue sauce
1 (3-lb.) frying chicken, cut up

Open a large, heavy paper bag (be sure there are no holes in it) and place it on its side on a large baking pan. With pastry brush, brush melted shortening over the inside of the bag, covering well. Place chicken pieces skin side up in a single layer on the bottom of the bag. Spoon barbecue sauce evenly over the chicken; fold the open end of the bag over twice and secure the closure with paper clips. Place the pan in a cold oven, then set the temperature control at 350 degrees, and bake the chicken for 1¾ hours. *Do not open* the bag during cooking time. Remove pan from oven and slit open the bag, remove chicken to a serving platter. Spoon sauce in the bag over the chicken and serve at once.

Wheel of Fortune

A supper has always been relied upon to replenish the treasury of any auxiliary, since such a fund-raising affair could be planned and staged within a few days, while a big summer sale required months of work. Suppers are of many types. Perhaps the best known and loved is a chicken-pie supper, although some men— like my father—looked on such with a distinctly jaundiced eye.

"I wouldn't mind going to one of the dang things," he'd explain to Mother, "if I could be sure of getting a piece of your pie. Or Alice B———'s. Or maybe any one of a half-dozen others. But somehow, it turns out I never do."

Mother admitted his extraordinarily bad luck at chicken-pie suppers. "I don't know why it is," she soothed him, "that you always get a slice of pie that doesn't have a blessed thing under the crust except a back and a wing."

One of our neighbors, a man of outspoken convictions, summed up the general feelings of the menfolk. This gentleman, after forking out a few bony and nondescript pieces of chicken, surveyed his fellow diners. "The Ladies Aid is dead set against any kind of gambling," he stated, "but what in tunket do they think a chicken-pie supper is? Biggest gamble on the face of the earth—at least as far as I'm concerned."

Country Chicken Pie

(For eight)

1 dressed fowl (*c.* 5 lbs.)	2 teaspoons salt
6 cups water	½ cup flour
1 medium onion, cut up	dash of pepper
2 stalks celery with leaves, cut up	

Place the fowl, water, onion and celery in a heavy kettle, cover and simmer for about 1 hour, then add 1 teaspoon of the salt. Cover and continue to simmer for 2 hours more, or until the meat is ready to fall from the bones. Remove the chicken and cool; strain the broth and skim off the fat. Cool ½ cup of the broth. Separate meat from bones and skin, leaving the meat in rather large pieces. Heat 3 cups of the broth to boiling; blend the flour smoothly with the ½ cup of cool broth. Stir into the boiling broth, beating well to prevent lumping. Add remaining 1 teaspoon of salt and the pepper. Combine the gravy with the meat, and turn into a round 9 x 3 baking dish. Cover with crust and bake in a 400 oven for about 45 minutes, or until brown and flaky. While the pie is baking, thicken the remaining broth to serve with the pie.

CRUST

1½ cups sifted flour	⅔ cup shortening
¾ teaspoon salt	about 4 tablespoons cold water

Sift the flour with the salt and rub in the shortening. Mix with just enough water to allow the pastry to be handled. Roll out on a floured board to about 10 inches in diameter—the crust should be a little thicker than for fruit pies. Place the crust over the chicken and turn the edges under; crimp. Slit the top several times to allow steam to escape. Bake as directed.

Some of the shortening can be solid chicken fat skimmed earlier from the broth.

Chicken à la King

(Six servings)

¼ cup minced green pepper	½ cup instant dry milk
1 small onion, peeled and minced	1 (4-oz.) can sliced mushrooms, drained
3 tablespoons melted butter or margarine	1½ cups diced cooked chicken
¼ cup flour	1 (2-oz.) jar diced pimientos, drained
1½ cups chicken broth	
2 chicken bouillon cubes	½ cup dairy soured cream

Simmer green pepper and onion for about 5 minutes in the melted butter, but do not allow the vegetables to brown. Stir in flour smoothly. Heat chicken broth to boiling point and add bouillon cubes. When cubes are dissolved, add the instant dry milk. Add this liquid to the flour-and-butter mixture, stirring over low heat until sauce boils and thickens. Add mushrooms and chicken and let all get very hot. Just before serving, stir in pimientos and soured cream. Heat again but *do not allow to boil.* Serve at once in patty shells, or over hot toast or hot biscuits. This is also excellent when served spooned over hot rice.

A delightful variation of an old standby. The soured cream makes all the difference.

Chicken Pie with Curry Sauce

(Six good servings)

1 frying chicken (*c.* 2½ lbs.), cut up	1 (10-oz.) package frozen peas, cooked and drained
3 cups water	1 canned pimiento, chopped
1 large stalk celery	4½ cups Curry Sauce
1 teaspoon salt	Milk Pastry
6 peppercorns	

Simmer the chicken in the water with celery, salt and peppercorns until tender. Remove chicken from broth and cool. Measure broth after straining. Add water, if necessary, to make 3 cups liquid. Remove skin, bones and fat from chicken. Cut meat in 1-inch pieces and combine with peas and pimiento. Stir in 2 cups of the Curry Sauce, reserving the remaining sauce to serve with the pie. Pour chicken and sauce mixture into 10 x 6 x 2 baking tin lined with Milk Pastry, and fit latticed pastry strips over top. Bake in a 400 oven for 20 minutes. Reduce heat to 350 and bake 35 minutes longer. Serve hot with reserved curry sauce spooned over each serving.

CURRY SAUCE

(About 4½ cups)

¾ stick margarine or butter, melted	pinch of pepper
6 tablespoons flour	1 teaspoon curry powder
1 teaspoon salt	3 cups chicken broth
	1 tall can evaporated milk, undiluted

Blend melted margarine, flour, salt, pepper and curry powder. Stir in the 3 cups chicken broth reserved from cooked chicken. Stir over low heat until smooth and thickened. Boil 1 minute, then add undiluted evaporated milk, blending well. Before serving, reheat remaining 2½ cups of sauce.

MILK PASTRY

2 cups sifted flour	⅓ cup shortening
1 teaspoon salt	⅔ cup milk

Sift flour with the salt, then rub in the shortening. Mix in the milk. Knead slightly on a floured board, then roll out ¼ inch thick. Line a baking pan, about 10 x 6 x 2. Use remaining pastry for lattice strips for top of pie.

Long Haul

For old-time suppers the women were quite ingenious in devising ways to keep things hot during the long trips in the surrey between house and community hall. I remember one who fashioned what she called a "hay-cooker." In a stout wooden box with a tight cover, she packed loose hay; she then set her covered hot dish down in a hollow in the hay, covered it with more hay, and fastened the box lid tight shut. Her food kept nice and hot until serving time.

Several women used "freestones" for the same purpose: soapstones heated to the right temperature on the kitchen range, then placed in a small metal tub. A pan of chicken pie or a pot of beans kept beautifully hot on the freestone.

Oven Fried Chicken #1

(Five or six servings)

2 (2-lb.) frying chickens	1¼ teaspoons seasoned salt
½ cup melted butter or margarine	1 medium onion, peeled and diced

Cut each chicken in serving pieces. Brush well with the melted butter and sprinkle with the seasoned salt. Place pieces skin side down in a baking pan; scatter diced onion over the top. Bake in a 375 oven for 30 minutes. Turn each piece and bake for 30 minutes longer, or until chicken is tender and brown.

Oven Fried Chicken #2

(Five or six servings)

2 (2-lb.) frying chickens
½ cup buttermilk
1 medium onion, peeled and minced
1 cup flour
2 teaspoons salt

¼ teaspoon pepper
2 teaspoons paprika
¼ teaspoon ground thyme
¼ cup butter or margarine

Cut chicken in serving pieces. Combine buttermilk and onion. Sift flour with the salt, pepper, paprika and thyme. Melt the butter in a baking pan. Brush each piece of chicken with the buttermilk mixture, then sprinkle generously with the seasoned flour. Place pieces skin side down in the baking pan, having turned each to coat it with the melted butter. Bake in a 375 oven for about 30 minutes, then turn each piece and bake 30 minutes longer, or until very tender.

Sweet and Tangy Chicken

(Four servings)

⅓ cup melted butter or margarine
3 tablespoons Worcestershire sauce
1 small clove garlic, peeled and
    minced
½ cup any tart red jelly

2 teaspoons prepared mustard
1 teaspoon sugar
3 drops Tabasco sauce
¼ teaspoon salt
1 frying chicken (3 lbs.), cut up

Combine all ingredients except chicken. Place over low heat and cook until jelly has melted and sauce has blended smoothly. Arrange chicken in a baking pan, skin side up. Pour sauce over evenly. Cover pan with foil and bake 30 minutes in a 400 oven; uncover pan and bake 30 minutes longer, or until chicken is tender and well browned. Baste with pan juices twice during last ½ hour of baking. Serve hot with the pan sauce spooned over each serving.

Chicken Breasts à l'Orange

(Eight servings)

8 large half breasts of chicken
2 tablespoons melted butter or
   margarine

flour, salt and pepper
8 large thin slices of peeled orange
Orange Sauce

Brush chicken with the melted butter, then dust lightly with flour, salt and pepper. Place skin side up in a baking pan, add ½ cup hot water. Cover and bake at 375 for 30 minutes; remove cover and bake 1 hour longer, or until chicken is very tender. Place one slice of orange on each breast and serve at once with Orange Sauce spooned over each serving.

This is a simply marvelous combination of flavors.

ORANGE SAUCE

(About two cups)

⅔ cup sugar
1 tablespoon cornstarch
½ teaspoon each of cinnamon,

ground cloves, salt
4 teaspoons grated orange rind
1 cup orange juice

Combine sugar, cornstarch, cinnamon, cloves, salt, grated rind and orange juice. Stir over low heat until smooth, thickened, and clear. Serve hot over each chicken breast.

Parson's Fare

Chicken was considered in years gone by as the only fitting food for special occasions. Since every farm boasted a varying assortment of poultry, there was always material at hand for any sudden emergency, such as asking the minister to stay for dinner when his parish call wasn't expected for at least another week.

I've often wondered if those reverend gentlemen ever got tired of the inevitable chicken served them at each home, no matter how succulent it might be. Perhaps they sometimes longed, instead, for fried salt pork and cream gravy with plain boiled potatoes.

Foil-baked Chicken, Rice and Cabbage

(Four servings)

1 frying chicken (2½ lbs.)	1 teaspoon salt
1 medium onion, peeled and minced	1 cup cooked rice
3 tablespoons melted butter or margarine	1 can cream of tomato soup, undiluted
3 cups shredded cabbage	1 cup fine dry breadcrumbs

Cut chicken in quarters. Simmer onion in the melted butter for 5 minutes. Add cabbage and simmer 10 minutes longer. Add salt, rice and undiluted soup, stirring as it heats. Have ready four pieces of aluminum foil, 12 x 12. Lightly oil one side and place a chicken quarter in the center of oiled side. Spoon rice and cabbage mixture evenly over the chicken; spread crumbs evenly over each top. Fold foil over and seal each package. Place on a baking pan and bake at 450 for about 35 minutes. Tear foil to expose crumbs and bake 15 minutes longer, or until browned. Serve at once.

A tasty and welcome change for chicken.

Baked Chicken Dinner

(Four good servings)

1 frying chicken (2 to 3 lbs.), cut up	1 cup buttermilk
2 tablespoons melted fat	¾ cup water
1 (6-oz.) package instant scalloped potatoes	¼ teaspoon salt
	small pinch of pepper
3 medium onions, peeled and sliced	

Brown chicken pieces in the melted fat, then place them in a baking dish. Arrange dried scalloped potatoes in and around the chicken, then shake over all the contents of the flavoring envelope. Lay onion slices over potatoes and chicken. Combine buttermilk and water and pour over the top, then sprinkle with the salt and pepper. Cover tightly and bake in a 350 oven until the chicken is very tender, about 1½ hours.

The whole dish is beautifully flavored; the buttermilk is not distinguishable, but is a subtle addition.

Jellied Chicken Loaf

(Six servings)

1 frying chicken (2 to 3 lbs.), cut up	2 cups hot water
1 large stalk celery	1 envelope plain gelatine
1 medium onion, peeled and quartered	¼ cup cold water
	¼ cup mayonnaise or salad dressing
2 teaspoons salt	2 teaspoons soy sauce
1 teaspoon ground ginger	½ cup finely chopped celery
8 peppercorns	1 large canned pimiento, minced

Place cut-up chicken in large kettle and add next six ingredients. Cover and simmer gently until chicken is very tender, about 1 hour. Remove chicken from broth and cool. Strain broth and add water, if needed, to make 2 cups of liquid. Soften the gelatine in the cold water, then add to the hot broth. Stir to dissolve, then remove from heat. Add mayonnaise and soy sauce. Cool, then chill until syrupy. When chicken is cool, remove skin, bones and fat. Chop meat fine and add to gelatine mixture. Add celery and pimiento. Pour into a 1½-quart loaf pan and refrigerate for several hours. Unmold on lettuce and garnish with sliced tomatoes. With hot rolls, it's a delicious summer luncheon.

This is a firm and meaty loaf with a creamy texture.

Mushroom-smothered Chicken

(Four servings)

1 frying chicken (2 to 3 lbs.)
1 teaspoon seasoned salt
small pinch of pepper
pinch of paprika
3 tablespoons cooking oil
1 medium onion, peeled and diced

2 tablespoons flour
¼ teaspoon poultry seasoning
1 cup milk
1 can cream of mushroom soup,
　　undiluted

Cut chicken in serving pieces, sprinkle each with the salt, pepper and paprika. Brown in the oil in a frying pan. Remove chicken and add diced onion to fat in the pan, cooking gently for 5 minutes. Mix flour and poultry seasoning and blend with pan mixture. Add milk, and stir over low heat until thickened. Add soup, stirring until well blended. Place chicken pieces in a baking dish, pour the sauce over them evenly, and cover and bake at 375 for about 1 hour, or until chicken is very tender. Baste with the sauce in the pan once or twice during baking time. Serve with pan sauce spooned over each serving.

Quick Paella

(Four to six servings)

2 tablespoons butter or margarine
2 tablespoons minced onion
1½ cups boiling water
2 chicken bouillon cubes
tiny pinch of saffron
1⅓ cups instant rice

1 (7-oz.) can minced clams,
　　undrained
1 (4-oz.) can shrimps, drained
2 cups chopped cooked chicken
2 canned pimientos, chopped
¼ teaspoon salt

Simmer butter and onion for 5 minutes over low heat. Add boiling water, bouillon cubes and saffron, stirring to dissolve the cubes. Add remaining ingredients, cover and simmer 5 minutes. Turn off heat and let mixture stand for about 15 minutes to allow flavors to blend.

Chicken Curry with Bananas

(Six servings)

1 small apple, peeled and chopped	1 tablespoon curry powder
1 medium onion, peeled and chopped	½ teaspoon salt
	1½ cups chicken broth
2 stalks celery, thinly sliced	½ cup milk
3 tablespoons melted butter or margarine	3 cups cut-up, cooked chicken
	2 bananas, slightly underripe
¼ cup flour	3 cups cooked rice

Simmer the apple, onion and celery in the melted butter for about 10 minutes, stirring occasionally: *do not brown.* Combine flour, curry powder and salt. Blend with mixture in frying pan. Combine chicken broth and milk, and pour into frying pan, stirring constantly. Stir over low heat until thickened. Add chicken. Peel bananas and cut in half lengthwise, then cut across in ¾-inch slices and add to chicken mixture. Heat very hot and serve at once with boiled rice.

A most attractive curry. The chicken makes a better appearance if it is pulled into pieces, rather than cut up.

Business Opportunity

Summer suppers were profitable, but presented problems in those days before insect sprays. Sheets of fly paper were laid out in places out of reach of the kitchen crew, but the flies ignored them in favor of lighting on spots nearer the food.

The answer was to have committee members bring their available children, even very little ones, armed with folded newspapers. The going rate for slaughtered flies was one cent for every corpse, although the price once in a while dropped to five cents a hundred. In any event, the promise of actual cash rewards usually resulted in nearly fly-free premises when the customers gathered.

Country Roast Turkey with Giblet Stuffing

(For fifteen)

1 oven-dressed turkey (10 to 12 lbs.)	8 cups stale bread cubes
1 teaspoon salt	chopped giblets
1 stalk celery with leaves, chopped	1½ teaspoons salt
¾ cup melted butter or margarine	1½ teaspoons poultry seasoning
1 cup chopped celery	hot water
1 cup chopped onions	

Wipe the turkey inside and out with a small cloth wrung from warm water. Refrigerate bird until ready to stuff.

Wash the giblets and put them in a small saucepan, add the neck, salt and celery stalk, covering well with hot water. Cover the pan and simmer until giblets are very tender. Drain and reserve broth. Cool the neck and giblets, pick meat from the neck and chop with the giblets rather fine. Sauté celery and onions in the butter until the onions are transparent, about 7 minutes. Combine with the bread cubes. Add chopped giblets to the bread mixture with the salt and poultry seasoning. Add enough hot water to hold the stuffing together lightly but not enough to make a wet mixture. Mix the stuffing lightly but well, and let cool. Salt the body and neck cavities of the turkey lightly and fill with stuffing: *do not pack tightly*. Close the openings with small skewers or sew with a heavy needle and thread. Slip the ends of drumsticks under the flap of skin under the tail or tie closely to body. Place on a rack in the roaster. Dip a square of white cloth—old sheeting is excellent—in melted unsalted shortening, and tuck in over the bird. Roast in a 325 oven for about 3 hours, or until your meat thermometer registers internal temperature at 185. No basting is necessary with cloth; if it dries out and turns brown, replace it with another.

Remove to a warm platter about 30 minutes before serving time to make carving easier.

GRAVY

(About 4 cups)

1¼ cups drippings	3 cups broth from giblets
½ cup flour	salt and pepper to taste

Blend the drippings smoothly with the flour, add broth from giblets and stir over low heat until smooth and thickened, then cook 1 minute longer. Season to taste with salt and pepper and serve in a gravy boat.

Turkey Chop Suey

(Six servings)

¼ cup butter or margarine	¼ cup cold water
2 cups sliced celery	1 tablespoon light molasses
2 cups green pepper strips	2 tablespoons soy sauce
1 cup thinly sliced onion	1 (5-oz.) can water chestnuts,
2 cups cooked turkey, cut in strips	drained
1½ cups boiling water	1 (1-lb.) can bean sprouts, drained
¼ teaspoon salt	about 3 cups cooked rice
2 tablespoons cornstarch	

Melt the butter in a large, heavy skillet. Add celery, green pepper, onion, turkey meat and the boiling water. Add salt, cover, then simmer for 15 minutes. Blend cornstarch smoothly with the cold water, then stir well into the vegetable-and-turkey mixture. Stir well, then add remaining ingredients. Bring to boiling point again, then simmer for 5 minutes. Serve with hot boiled rice.

Looking Ahead

One of the hardest-working women I ever knew took a prominent part in putting on community suppers. At home, she worked

incessantly caring for a large house and numerous family mem-
bers. Folks often remarked that they just didn't see how Agnes
E—— did so much "and her not in too good health."

At one supper, she confided to the other women working in the
kitchen that she had been to the doctor over in Lyme. "He said if
I don't let up, I'm going to have a nervous breakdown." She stood
there with a wistful look on her face. "You know, I've always
wanted to have one of those nervous breakdowns. But every time I
thought I could spare the time, something would come up that
needed doing and I'd have to put it off."

Turkey-Sausage Puff

(Six to eight servings)

1 pound bulk sausage	2 cups soft breadcrumbs
½ cup minced onion	1 teaspoon poultry seasoning
1 cup diced celery	3 cups leftover turkey gravy
2 eggs, beaten	2 cups diced, cooked turkey
1 cup milk	salt and pepper to taste

Cook the sausage over moderate heat until nearly done but not
browned, breaking the meat apart with a fork. Pour off the fat,
leaving about 2 tablespoons in the pan; add onion and celery and
continue cooking for about 5 minutes. Combine beaten eggs,
milk, breadcrumbs, poultry seasoning and 1 cup of the gravy.
Stir in the turkey. Taste and add salt and pepper as needed. Stir
in the sausage mixture, turn into a greased 10 x 7 baking pan, and
bake in a 350 oven for about 45 minutes, or until set and browned.
Remove from the oven and let stand 10 minutes. Serve with remaining gravy, heated.

An extremely tasty way to use leftover turkey or chicken.

Salmon and Broccoli Casserole

(Six servings)

2 (10-oz.) packages frozen broccoli
1 (1-lb.) can red salmon, drained
2 cups medium white sauce
4 teaspoons lemon juice

1 teaspoon Worcestershire sauce
¼ cup grated Parmesan cheese
¼ cup cornflake crumbs
pinch of paprika

Cook broccoli according to package directions. Drain, and arrange in a buttered casserole. Remove bones and skin from salmon, flaking the fish, and place it over the broccoli. Combine white sauce, lemon juice, Worcestershire sauce; spread over the salmon. Combine grated cheese and the cornflake crumbs, spread evenly over the top, and sprinkle with the paprika. Bake uncovered in a 350 oven until bubbling hot and browned, about 35 minutes.

Friends Indeed

Neighborly help has always been an integral part of any women's society program, although it brings in not one cent to swell the treasury. At one time or another, most families have emergencies, and food brought in at those periods is both aid and comfort.

The food is chosen carefully. For instance, the new widower with a large brood receives hearty dishes different from those brought to an elderly spinster who could very easily buy all she needs. In the former case, hash, meat or fish casseroles, chowder, scalloped potatoes, spaghetti or macaroni with sauces, cakes and pies—anything, in short, that is home-cooked, nutritious, and easy to serve. In the latter case, the foods are more on the order of delicacies, to show attention and respect.

If the emergency is likely to be of some duration, a schedule is drawn up for the ladies to take turns providing the main dishes. In the same manner the members of the society will organize the repast that is served after a funeral to out-of-town friends and relatives. I know of one touching instance when the post-funeral meals were so well planned for that a thoughtful neighbor quietly undertook to wash and iron the children's school clothes until the bereaved household could establish a routine again.

Fish and Vegetable Casserole

(For six)

1 (12-oz.) package frozen fish fillets	1 cup milk
3 medium potatoes, peeled and diced	3 tablespoons melted butter
3 medium carrots, peeled and diced	3 tablespoons flour
3 medium onions, peeled and thinly sliced	½ teaspoon seasoned salt
1 teaspoon salt	pinch of pepper
1½ cups water	1 recipe Buttermilk Biscuits (*see* Breads)
1 chicken bouillon cube	

Place the vegetables, water and salt in a kettle, cover and simmer until almost tender. Cut thawed fish in 1-inch pieces and add. When all is tender, remove from heat and drain, reserving the liquid. Measure liquid and add hot water to make 1½ cups in all. Add the bouillon cube and stir to dissolve; add milk. Blend melted butter and flour, then blend in the milk mixture, stirring over low heat until smooth and thickened. Combine with fish mixture, stirring just enough to mix, then turn into a greased casserole and place cut biscuits over the top. Bake in a 400 oven for about 25 minutes. Let stand 10 minutes before serving.

Shrimp, Egg and Rice Casserole

(Six servings)

6 hard-cooked eggs, shelled	½ cup milk
¼ cup creamy salad dressing	½ cup dairy soured cream
2 teaspoons prepared mustard	1 (5-oz.) can shrimps, drained
½ teaspoon salt	2 tablespoons grated Parmesan
4 cups freshly boiled rice, drained	cheese
1 can frozen cream of shrimp soup, thawed	paprika

Cut eggs in half crossways. Mash yolks and blend well with salad dressing, mustard and salt, and fill the whites with the mixture. Place the rice in a shallow buttered casserole, and arrange egg halves evenly on the rice, pushing gently down. Combine the soup with the milk and soured cream, stirring over moderate heat until well blended, add the shrimps and pour over eggs and rice. Sprinkle with the grated cheese, then dust with paprika. Bake in a 375 oven for about 30 minutes, or until lightly browned and bubbling hot.

Emergency Rations

Potluck suppers belong in a category all to themselves. If some men used to consider a chicken-pie supper a gamble, surely a potluck meal is even more of a lottery. The prospective diner can only guess what luck will bring to his particular table.

Each family contributes something to the meal. It may be a meat casserole, a pie, a salad, perhaps a jar of pickles. Strangely enough, these affairs always seem to turn out pretty well as to variety. Only once over the years have I been disappointed. And that was during wartime when lots of foods were pretty scarce, even in rural Vermont.

That night there were perhaps thirty or forty families assembled for the supper. Each group brought a dish, some families more than one, and, believe it or not, every single offering turned out to be some variation of a spaghetti or macaroni casserole.

Baked Bean and Apple Casserole

(Six servings)

2 cups dried navy beans
⅔ teaspoon salt
2 medium apples, peeled, cored and

sliced
½ cup light brown sugar
¼ pound fat salt pork, sliced

Soak beans overnight in water, covering well. In the morning, drain and just barely cover in fresh water. Add salt, cover and simmer about 1 hour, or until beans are just tender. Drain, reserving liquid. In heavy casserole make alternate layers of the beans and the sliced apples, ending with a bean layer. Sprinkle each layer with a part of the brown sugar. Lay the salt pork slices on top of the beans. Pour in the reserved bean liquid just to the level of the top layer of beans. Cover and bake in a 350 oven for about 2 hours—the longer they bake, the better they'll be. If the beans appear dry during baking, add a little more of the reserved liquid, so the beans are rather moist when done.

The apples make such a nice variation.

Green Pea Casserole with Carrot Sauce

(Four servings)

2 cups cooked green peas
1 cup soft breadcrumbs
1 teaspoon grated onion
pinch each of salt and pepper

1 tablespoon sugar
1¼ cups hot milk
2 eggs, beaten

Rub peas through a coarse sieve; add breadcrumbs, onion, salt, pepper, sugar, milk and beaten eggs. Mix gently and turn into a buttered 1-quart casserole and bake covered in a 350 oven for about 50 minutes, or until set. Serve with hot Carrot Sauce spooned over each portion.

The lovely-colored sauce is a perfect complement to the pale green of the casserole.

Carrot Sauce

2 tablespoons butter or margarine	2 cups cooked carrots
2 tablespoons flour	salt and pepper to taste
1½ cups milk	

Blend flour into melted butter, add milk and stir over low heat until smooth and thickened. Rub the carrots through a coarse sieve and add; season to taste with salt and pepper. Heat and serve.

Lima Bean and Sausage Bake

(Four servings)

1 cup dried baby lima beans	tiny pinch of pepper
¾ teaspoon salt	2 tablespoons minced onion
½ pound bulk sausage	2 tablespoons minced green pepper
¼ teaspoon poultry seasoning	1 cup undiluted evaporated milk

Soak lima beans overnight in water just covering. In the morning, set over moderate heat and add salt; cover, and simmer until beans are just tender, about 1 hour. Drain. Cook sausage until lightly browned, breaking meat apart with fork. Drain off the fat, then add the sausage to the beans. Add poultry seasoning and pepper, then stir in the onion and green pepper. Turn into a buttered casserole and add the milk. Cover and bake about 45 minutes in a 325 oven.

Land of Plenty

Although sometimes a collection is taken, there is usually no admission charged for potluck suppers in my area, since they are more often designed for good fellowship than to raise money. Per-

haps this is why large families have always turned out heavily for such functions.

I remember particularly one family which numbered eight or ten children, an overworked wife and a husband who provided rather haphazardly for his brood. They would arrive early and take over the whole end of one long table, the wife placing their contribution—often a small dish of scalloped potatoes—in the center of the table. After the minister asked the blessing, the father always called out jovially to his offspring: "Pitch in, kids! Remember, it's free!" To show that this was humor, he'd guffaw and slap the shoulder of the nearest diner, be it man or woman.

And pitch in they did. As Mother said, "Land sakes, it does my heart good to see those poor children stuff themselves."

Chicken Liver and Spaghetti Bake

(For six)

¾ pound hamburger
2 small onions, chopped
1 large green pepper, seeded and
    chopped
2 tablespoons vegetable oil
1 (1-lb.) can tomatoes, undrained
1 (6-oz.) can tomato paste
1 teaspoon ground basil

1 teaspoon chili powder
1 teaspoon salt
small dash of cayenne pepper
1 pound chicken livers, cut up
2 tablespoons melted butter or
    margarine
½ pound thin spaghetti

Simmer hamburger, onions, green pepper and oil until meat has lost its red color. Rub tomatoes through a sieve and add; add the tomato paste, then stir in the seasonings. Cover and simmer over very low heat for about 1 hour, stirring occasionally. Simmer the chicken livers and butter for 10 minutes, stirring. Add to hamburger mixture. Cook spaghetti according to package directions, drain and place in buttered 2-quart baking dish. Pour meat sauce over the spaghetti and mix lightly with a fork. Cover and bake in a 350 oven for 30 minutes.

One of the best spaghetti dishes I know.

Chicken-Mushroom-Barley Casserole

(Five to six servings)

1 large onion, peeled and diced	3 cups chicken broth
½ pound fresh mushrooms, sliced	1½ cups cubed cooked chicken
¼ cup melted butter or margarine	½ teaspoon salt
1 cup pearl barley	pinch of pepper

Cook onion and mushrooms in the melted butter slowly until tender, about 10 minutes; add barley and continue cooking until slightly browned. Add broth, chicken, salt and pepper. Mix all well, then turn into a greased 2-quart casserole. Cover and bake in a 350 oven about 1 hour, or until broth is nearly absorbed and barley is tender.

The barley makes an interesting change from rice or macaroni.

Chicken and Sausage Casserole

(Six to eight servings)

3 (2-oz.) envelopes dry chicken-noodle soup mix	1 medium green pepper, seeded and chopped
1 cup raw rice	4 stalks celery, sliced
6 cups water	1 can cream of mushroom soup, undiluted
1 pound bulk sausage	
1 medium onion, chopped	

Combine soup mix, rice and water; cover and simmer for 30 minutes. Cook sausage over moderate heat until lightly browned, breaking meat apart with a fork. Pour off the fat, leaving about 1 tablespoonful in the pan. Remove the rice mixture from the heat and add the sausage to it. Put the vegetables in the fat remaining in the pan and simmer for 10 minutes, then add to sausage and rice. Turn the mixture into a greased 2-quart casserole; cover and bake in a 375 oven for about 40 minutes.

Country Pilau

(For six)

1 cup brown rice	2 tablespoons minced onion
2½ cups boiling water	½ pound fresh mushrooms, sliced
2 chicken bouillon cubes	½ pound chicken livers, quartered
½ pound bulk sausage	¼ teaspoon salt
3 tablespoons margarine or butter	pinch of pepper

Cook the rice in the boiling water, to which the bouillon cubes have been added; cover the pot and cook slowly for about 30 minutes, or until water is almost all absorbed. Fry the sausage gently until nearly done, breaking the meat apart with a fork. Pour off the fat and add the margarine, onion, mushrooms and livers. Cover and cook about 10 minutes, stirring frequently, until livers have lost any red color. Add salt and pepper. Combine the rice and the meat mixture and place in a buttered 1½-quart baking dish. Cover and bake in a 400 oven for about 20 minutes. Serve hot.

This wonderfully tasty Southern dish is a favorite in our Vermont household.

Baked Casserole of Liver

(Four to six servings)

1 pound baby beef liver, sliced	1 teaspoon poultry seasoning
2 tablespoons flour	5 medium potatoes, peeled and
1 teaspoon salt	sliced
pinch of pepper	1 cup boiling water
1 large onion, peeled and diced	1 chicken bouillon cube
2 medium apples, peeled and diced	

Cut liver into serving pieces. Combine flour, salt and pepper and use all the mixture to dredge meat thoroughly. Combine onion, apples and poultry seasoning. In a buttered casserole, place half the liver, cover with half the apple-onion mixture, then cover with half the potatoes. Repeat layers. Dissolve the bouillon cube in boiling water and pour over all. Cover and bake in a 375 oven for about 1 hour, or until tender and broth is partially absorbed.

Beef and Sausage Casserole

(Six servings)

½ pound hamburger	½ cup chopped green pepper
½ pound bulk sausage	¼ cup grated Parmesan cheese
1 (4-oz.) can mushrooms	½ teaspoon salt
3 chicken bouillon cubes	¼ teaspoon marjoram
water	pinch of pepper
½ cup chopped celery	1 cup uncooked rice

Combine hamburger and sausage and stir over low heat until lightly browned; pour off the fat. Drain the mushrooms; reserve the liquid, and add enough water to it to make 3 cups in all, heat to boiling and in it dissolve the bouillon cubes. Add celery, green pepper, cheese and mushrooms to the meat. Season with the salt, marjoram and pepper. Add the broth. Stir to mix, then add the rice. Pour into a buttered 2-quart casserole. Cover and bake in a 375 oven for about 1 hour, or until rice is tender.

Self-Help

Henry W—— was expected to contribute generously to every supper, it being the common belief that all storekeepers were rolling in money. Some of the folks suspected, though, that "Hen's" business was done principally on credit, a good deal of it pretty elusive.

One farmer, notoriously poor pay, came in regularly to trade, and after being asked to settle his bill, began paying cash for what he got. Each time he'd say, "I'm going to begin paying something on that old bill before long, Hen. I swear, it's run long enough."

And when he had left the store, Hen would jot something down in his ledger.

"What are you setting down?" Grandfather asked once. "He paid for what he got and he never gave you a cent on the old bill that I could see."

"Well," replied the storekeeper, "every time he duns himself, I knock ten cents off that old bill."

Curried Ham and Rice Casserole

(Six servings)

1 can cream of chicken soup, undiluted	1½ cups cooked rice
½ cup undiluted evaporated milk	1 (1-lb.) can whole green beans, drained
½ cup dairy soured cream	1 (2-oz.) can pimientos, drained and chopped
2 teaspoons dry minced onion	1 cup cooked ham strips
1 teaspoon curry powder	

Combine soup, milk and soured cream; stir until smooth, then add onion and curry powder. Add rice, green beans, pimientos and ham, stirring just enough to mix. Turn into a greased 1½-quart casserole, cover and bake in a 325 oven for about 50 minutes.

A good grade of canned luncheon meat, cut into thin strips, may be used instead of ham in this really good casserole.

Sour Cream, Potato and Ham Casserole

(Six servings)

1 cup dairy soured cream	1 cup ground cooked ham
½ cup undiluted evaporated milk	¾ cup fine dry breadcrumbs
1 teaspoon instant minced onion	2 tablespoons melted butter or margarine
6 medium potatoes, cooked and sliced	¼ teaspoon seasoned salt
3 hard-cooked eggs, sliced	

Blend soured cream with milk and onion. Place ⅓ of the potato slices in buttered 1½-quart casserole, cover with the sliced eggs, and cover the eggs with ½ the cream mixture. Cover with ½ the remaining potato slices, then spread the ham over them. Cover the ham with remaining soured cream mixture, then the remaining potato slices. Combine crumbs, melted butter and seasoned salt, and sprinkle over top. Bake uncovered in a 350 oven for about 45 minutes, or until sauce is bubbling hot and the crumbs are browned.

Baked Cheese-Ham Casserole

(Six to eight servings)

2 cups elbow macaroni	3 cups milk
2 tablespoons butter or margarine	3 eggs
2 tablespoons grated onion	½ teaspoon Worcestershire sauce
1 (12-oz.) can luncheon meat, diced	¼ cup grated Parmesan cheese
1 cup shredded sharp cheese (¼ lb.)	paprika

Cook the macaroni according to package directions; drain. While it is still hot, stir in the butter and onion, then add the diced meat. Stir in the shredded cheese. Beat the milk and eggs together with the Worcestershire sauce. Place the macaroni mixture in a buttered 2-quart casserole, then pour the milk mixture over it. Sprinkle the top with the Parmesan cheese and dust lightly with paprika. Bake, uncovered, in a 350 oven for about 1 hour.

This may be served at once but is even better after standing a short while. It can be re-heated successfully.

Luncheon Supper

Motivation

When it became sadly evident, some years ago, that the sewing just wasn't going to get done on time, someone came up with the idea that the Work Committee do all the actual sewing for the big summer sale. Committee members would be appointed by the president, and would be the hardest-working and best needle-women in the whole Society.

The plan worked. The committee met early and late, and as sale-time drew near, two or three sessions a week often were necessary. Even so, a number of women actually asked to be added to the committee.

Why did it work? Because the ladies were assured of a delectable array of good things to eat while plying needles and scissors, since each hostess in turn used new and elegant recipes—ones too expensive or elaborate to serve for the big monthly meetings.

Gourmet Hamburgers

(For eight)

2 pounds good ground beef	½ cup minced onion
¼ cup crumbled Blue cheese	8 hamburger buns, toasted

Divide meat into 16 equal portions. Flatten each with the hand into a thin patty. Combine cheese and onion. Spread evenly over 8 of the patties. Cover with remaining patties. Seal edges with the fingers. Grill as usual and serve on the hot toasted buns.

Grilled Chicken Salad Sandwiches

(For four)

1½ cups finely chopped cooked
  chicken
¾ cup finely chopped celery
¼ teaspoon salt
2 well-drained canned pineapple
  slices

⅓ cup mayonnaise or salad dressing
8 slices bread
¼ cup melted butter or margarine
¼ cup seasoned coating mix for
  chicken

Combine the chicken, celery and salt. Cut the pineapple slices in thin slivers and add to the chicken mixture along with the mayonnaise. Spread over 4 slices of the bread, then cover with the remaining slices. Brush both sides of each sandwich with the melted butter, using any remaining butter to grease the griddle. Sprinkle the coating mix evenly over both sides of each sandwich. Grill on a moderately hot griddle until outside is nicely browned and the inside bubbling hot. Serve at once.

A marvelous hot main-dish sandwich.

Hot Tuna Puffs

(Six large sandwiches)

6 slices bread
1 (7-oz.) can tuna, drained
2 teaspoons minced onion
1 teaspoon prepared mustard

½ teaspoon Worcestershire sauce
½ cup mayonnaise or salad dressing
1 beaten egg
¼ cup shredded cheese

Place the bread on a broiler pan and toast lightly on *only one* side. Blend the tuna, onion, mustard, Worcestershire sauce and ¼ cup of the mayonnaise. Spread evenly over the untoasted side of each bread slice. Blend the beaten egg, cheese and remaining mayonnaise, and spread over the tuna mixture. Return to the lowest shelf of the broiler until gently brown and the topping looks puffy. Serve at once.

Quick Biscuit Pizza

(For six to eight)

1 pound bulk sausage
1 (6-oz.) can tomato paste
1 (8-oz.) can tomato sauce
1 teaspoon oregano
small dash of cayenne pepper

2 tubes ready-to-bake biscuits
  (about 20)
1 cup shredded sharp cheese (¼ lb.)
¼ cup grated Parmesan cheese

Cook sausage over moderate heat until nearly done, breaking meat apart with a fork. Drain off fat, add to the sausage the tomato paste, tomato sauce, oregano and cayenne. Rinse tomato cans with about ¼ cup hot water and add. Stir to mix and simmer 15 minutes. Open biscuits and flatten with the fingers until each is about 4 inches in diameter. Place on a greased large cookie pan, pulling each biscuit until all fit together nicely. Spread with the sauce, sprinkle on the shredded cheese, then top with the Parmesan. Bake in a 425 oven for about 20 minutes, or until nicely browned and bubbling hot.

Eggs with Smoked Oysters

(Four to six servings)

8 eggs
½ teaspoon salt
¼ teaspoon pepper

¼ cup light cream
1 tin smoked oysters, drained

Beat eggs slightly, only enough to break the yolks. Add salt, pepper and cream. Drain oil from oysters and pour into skillet. Heat, tipping pan until bottom and sides of pan are coated with the oil. Pour off any excess oil. Pour egg mixture into heated pan and scramble. When eggs are half done, add oysters. Continue cooking until eggs are set. Serve at once.

Pennsylvania Dutch Egg Bread

(Four to six servings)

3 slices stale bread, crusts removed   ¼ teaspoon salt
¼ cup melted margarine or butter   pinch of pepper
6 eggs

Cut bread in ½-inch cubes. Place butter in heavy skillet. Add bread cubes and stir to coat each with the butter. Cook over moderate heat until bread cubes are crisp and golden brown. Beat eggs slightly to mix yolks and whites, stir in the salt and pepper and pour over the bread cubes. Continue cooking until eggs are set. Turn when bottom is brown, as with an omelet. Serve at once when other side has browned.

Onion-smothered Eggs

(For four)

¼ cup butter or margarine   8 eggs
2 teaspoons Worcestershire sauce   salt and pepper to taste
2 medium onions, diced

Melt butter in a large frying pan. Stir in the Worcestershire sauce, add onions, and cook very slowly until tender and golden brown, stirring occasionally. With a spoon, make 8 shallow beds in the onion mixture. Break 1 egg into each bed, being very careful not to break the yolks. Cover and cook over very low heat until eggs are set. Sprinkle the eggs with a little salt and pepper to suit individual tastes. Serve on hot toast.

Catering Service

Enterprising auxiliaries discovered long ago that there was money to be made by putting on meals for special groups. There were few catering services in years gone by and women's societies filled a real need in both small communities and large.

Today they've found that serving the regular luncheon or dinner for Rotary, Kiwanis, Lions or other service organizations is a steady source of revenue. Or the meal may be for some local convention, for the annual teachers' meeting or a large summertime auction. These affairs are no more work than a regular supper and show a satisfying profit for the effort.

The ladies expertly choose the menu to suit the sort of group to be catered, balancing the amount of money it's willing to pay with the foods that will show the most clear profit. The main dish, the meat course, usually has to be purchased: after all, it's not easy to solicit a roast beef or a whole baked ham.

However, there are wonderful recipes available to any community group for making the most of lower-cost meats. I heard one such committee member point out that men were apt to be satisfied with whatever was put on the table if it was good and there was plenty of it. In general, I've found this to be true.

Creamy Cheese and Vegetables

(Six servings)

1 medium green pepper, diced	1 canned pimiento, diced
2 large stalks celery, diced	1 (4-oz.) can mushrooms, undrained
3 tablespoons butter or margarine	1 cup shredded sharp cheese (4 oz.)
3 tablespoons flour	½ teaspoon Worcestershire sauce
1½ cups milk	2 drops Tabasco sauce
2 cups cooked green peas	5 hard-cooked eggs, quartered

Cook the green pepper and celery gently in the butter for 10 minutes. Blend in the flour, add the milk, and stir over low heat until thickened. Add peas, pimiento, mushrooms, cheese, Worcestershire sauce and Tabasco. Stir until cheese has melted. Heat very hot, then add eggs, and salt if desired. Don't boil. Serve at once in Patty Shells, or with hot rice or toast points.

Asparagus and Cheese Soufflé

(For four)

¼ cup melted butter or margarine
¼ cup flour
1 cup milk
⅓ cup Roquefort (or Blue) cheese

4 eggs, separated
1 cup cooked sliced asparagus
¼ teaspoon cream of tartar

Blend melted butter and flour. Add milk. Stir over low heat until smooth and thick. Add cheese and stir until melted. Beat egg yolks until fluffy, then add the hot sauce very gradually, beating constantly. Add asparagus. Beat egg whites and cream of tartar until stiff, then fold in. Bake in a 350 oven in buttered baking dish for about 1 hour. Serve at once.

The Roquefort is the gourmet touch to this superb soufflé.

Tomatoes, Cheese and Eggs

(Four servings)

2 tablespoons melted fat
2 tablespoons minced onion
1 cup undrained canned tomatoes
½ teaspoon salt
½ teaspoon sugar

dash of pepper
few grains cayenne
½ cup shredded sharp cheese
    (2 oz.)
4 eggs

Cook fat and onion gently together for 5 minutes, then add to-matoes, salt, sugar, pepper and cayenne. Cover and simmer 10 minutes. Stir in cheese. Break eggs evenly spaced into tomato-cheese mixture, taking care not to break yolks. Cover and cook over very low heat until eggs are set, about 10 minutes. Serve on hot toast with the sauce spooned over and around eggs.

Mushroom Pie

(Four to six servings)

1 medium onion, peeled and diced
2 tablespoons butter or margarine
1 (4-oz.) can sliced mushrooms,
    drained
3 eggs, slightly beaten

1 cup dairy soured cream
1/4 teaspoon paprika
small pinch of pepper
1/2 teaspoon salt
unbaked 9-inch Pie Shell (*see* Pies)

Simmer onion and butter for 5 minutes, then add mushrooms. Beat eggs, soured cream, paprika, pepper and salt, add to mushroom mixture, and remove pan from heat. Bake the Pie Shell for about 8 minutes in a 400 oven. Remove from the oven and fill with the mushroom mixture. Return to the oven, reduce heat to 350 and bake about 30 minutes, or until filling is set and slightly browned. Let stand out of the oven for 10 minutes before serving. Cut in wedges.

Hamburger and Mushroom Pie

(Five to six servings)

1 small onion, peeled and chopped
1 tablespoon melted fat
1 pound hamburger
1 can cream of mushroom soup,
    undiluted

1/2 teaspoon seasoned salt
1 teaspoon Worcestershire sauce
Pie Pastry for 2 crusts (*see* Pies)

Simmer onion in the melted fat for about 5 minutes. Add the hamburger and cook over low heat, stirring until the meat has lost its red color. Add soup, salt and Worcestershire sauce. Mix all well, then pour into a pastry-lined pie tin. Cover with top crust, seal edges and make several slits in the center of the top. Bake in a 400 oven for about 45 minutes. Remove from the oven and let stand for 10 minutes before serving.

Mushrooms à la King

(For six)

½ pound fresh mushrooms, sliced
4 tablespoons melted butter or
    margarine
4 tablespoons flour
2 cups milk
½ teaspoon salt
pinch of paprika

½ teaspoon Worcestershire sauce
3 hard-cooked eggs, sliced
¼ cup sliced stuffed olives
1 cup sliced celery, cooked until
    just barely tender
¼ cup grated sharp cheese

Simmer mushrooms in the butter for 5 minutes. Blend in the flour, then add the milk. Stir over low heat until smooth and thick. Add salt, paprika and Worcestershire sauce. Add eggs, olives and celery. Stir in the cheese. Cover and cook over very low heat for about 15 minutes. Serve with hot rice, waffles, or fill Patty Shells (*see* Pie Pastry) or toast cups.

Delicate Chicken Mold

(Four generous servings)

1 undiluted can chicken and rice
    soup
1 (3-oz.) package cream cheese
1 tablespoon unflavored gelatine
¼ cup cold water

1 teaspoon lemon juice
2 drops Tabasco sauce
½ cup minced celery
¼ cup mayonnaise or salad dressing

Combine soup and cream cheese. Stir over low heat until well blended. Soften the gelatine in the cold water, add it to the soup mixture and stir until gelatine has dissolved. Remove from heat and add the lemon juice and Tabasco. Cool. Add celery and mayonnaise. Stir until blended. Turn into 4 or 5 individual molds. Chill until firm. Unmold on lettuce. If desired, garnish with additional mayonnaise, although it really is not needed.

This is a favorite recipe—inexpensive, most delicious, and can be prepared in a couple of minutes. An ideal main-dish salad for a Work Committee lunch.

Chicken Livers in Mushroom-Sour Cream Sauce

(Four to six servings)

1 pound chicken livers	undiluted
3 tablespoons vegetable oil	1 cup dairy soured cream
3 tablespoons diced onion	salt and pepper to taste
1 can cream of mushroom soup,	3 cups cooked rice or noodles

Simmer oil and onion for about 5 minutes. Cut livers in about 3 pieces each, add to onions and cook for 15 minutes more, turning occasionally. Add mushroom soup and stir to mix. Cover pan and cook very slowly for about 30 minutes; stir to prevent sticking. Add soured cream, stir well and season to taste with salt and pepper. Heat very hot but do not boil after adding soured cream. Leave over very low heat for about 10 minutes so that flavors may blend. Serve with boiled rice or noodles.

Chicken Liver-stuffed Pancake Rolls

(For four to six)

½ pound chicken livers	margarine
1½ cups water	5 tablespoons flour
1 chicken bouillon cube	½ teaspoon salt
1 cup milk	small pinch of pepper
4 tablespoons melted butter or	

Cook livers in the water, to which the bouillon cube has been added. When tender (after about 15 minutes), drain, reserving the broth. Cut up livers coarsely. To 1 cup of the broth, add the milk. Blend melted butter and the flour, add the broth and milk, and stir over low heat until smooth and thick. Add salt and pepper. To the cut-up livers, add enough of the sauce, about ¾ cup, to make rather moist. Keep hot, also keeping remainder of the sauce hot, as well. Make Thin Pancakes (below). Place a spoonful of the liver mixture in the center of each cake when it is done, roll and keep hot. Serve with the reserved sauce spooned over each portion.

THIN PANCAKES

(Eight to ten)

¾ cup sifted flour	2 eggs, beaten
½ teaspoon salt	⅔ cup milk
1 teaspoon baking powder	⅓ cup water

Sift dry ingredients into a bowl; add beaten eggs, milk and water all at once. Mix with a few rapid strokes but don't beat. Brush a 5-inch frying pan with a little oil and place over heat. When hot, add just enough of the batter to cover the bottom of the pan with a thin coating—tip the pan from side to side to spread batter evenly. Cook over moderate heat, turning pancake when browned on under side. Grease pan between each cake.

Quick Chicken (or Turkey) Tarts

(For ten)

1 cup minced cooked chicken	½ teaspoon poultry seasoning
½ cup minced celery	salt to taste
2 tablespoons grated onion	2 tubes refrigerator biscuits
2 tablespoons mayonnaise	

Combine the chicken, celery, onion, mayonnaise and poultry seasoning, and add salt to taste. Open the biscuit tubes and flatten each biscuit into a 5-inch circle with the palm of the hand. Place 10 circles on a greased cookie pan, put equal amounts of the chicken mixture in the center of each circle, and cover with another circle. Pinch the edges together to seal and prick the tops with a fork. Bake in a 400 oven for about 15 minutes.

Sausage-Eggplant Jumble

(For four)

2/3 pound bulk sausage
1 clove garlic, minced
1 medium green pepper, diced
3 fresh tomatoes, peeled and cut up
1 medium onion, diced

1 peeled medium eggplant, cubed
1 teaspoon sugar
pinch of salt
dash of pepper

Slice sausage and quarter each slice (or form 1¼-inch patties). Fry gently on both sides until partially cooked. Pour off the fat, add garlic, green pepper, tomatoes, onion and eggplant, and sprinkle with the sugar, salt and pepper. Cover and cook over low heat, stirring occasionally, until the eggplant is tender, about 30 minutes. Serve hot with mashed potatoes or rice.

Peas in Patty Shells

(For six)

2 tablespoons melted butter or
  margarine
1 small onion, minced
pinch of salt
small dash of pepper
½ teaspoon sugar
3 tablespoons flour

1 cup milk
1 cup dairy soured cream
1 tablespoon lemon juice
about 2 cups cooked green peas,
  well drained
6 Patty Shells (*see* **Pie Pastry**)

Simmer butter and onion until golden. Add salt, pepper and sugar. Blend in flour. Add milk. Stir over very low heat until smooth and thick. Stir in soured cream and lemon juice; add peas. Heat very hot, but do not boil. Fill Patty Shells and serve at once.

Garden Medley

(Six servings)

⅓ cup butter or margarine
1 small onion, peeled and grated
⅓ cup flour
2 cups milk
1 cup chicken broth
1 teaspoon salt
pinch of pepper

1 (4-oz.) can sliced mushrooms, drained
2 cups cooked asparagus
2 cups cooked green peas
2 cups cooked sliced carrots
1 beaten egg yolk

Melt butter in heavy skillet, add the onion and blend in the flour. Combine milk and broth and add; stir over low heat until smooth and thick. Season with the salt and pepper. Add the vegetables. Stir ¼ cup of the hot sauce into the beaten egg yolk, then add all to the mixture in the skillet. Heat very hot but don't boil. Serve over hot toast, biscuits or rice.

Efficiency Expert

Mrs. Maudie P—— served for many years as president of the local women's society, and very ably, too. Some called her a little heavy-handed in ramming through a vote for a pet project, but one and all agreed that when it came to getting things done, Maudie P—— couldn't be beaten.

For instance, there was the time she was on an important committee, whose responsibility it was to investigate and to select the proper places for fixtures when the town got electricity and the women raised money to wire the parsonage. When the committee met at the parsonage on the appointed day, they found the fixtures all installed, the places having been se-

lected by Maudie, who had overseen the work the day before. After all, she always maintained, the best committee in the world is the one that has three members and two of them stay home.

Stuffed Bacon Roll

(Four to six servings)

1 pound lean bacon slices
4 cups croûton-type dry poultry
   stuffing

¼ cup minced onion
¼ cup minced celery
boiling water

Separate the bacon slices and lay them on a sheet of waxed paper with the edges of the slices overlapping slightly—by about ½ inch—to form a rectangular layer, 14 x 9. Combine the dry stuffing, onion, and celery; add the boiling water according to package directions. Shape into a roll about 9 inches long. Place crossways of the bacon slices, bring ends of the bacon slices up around the roll of stuffing, overlapping the ends. Place, overlapping side down, on a wire rack in a baking pan, and bake 1 hour in a 375 oven. Serve with Pan Gravy if desired.

Pan Gravy

3 tablespoons flour
3 tablespoons pan juices
1 cup boiling water

1 onion bouillon cube
½ cup milk

Stir the flour into the pan juices, add the boiling water and the bouillon cube. Stir over low heat until all is dissolved, smooth and thick, then add the milk. Stir 1 minute longer, and serve.

Swiss-Ham-Rice Salad

(Six servings)

2 cups cooked rice, well drained
2 tablespoons finely minced onion
2 cups cooked green peas, drained
1 cup slivered Swiss cheese (¼ lb.)

1 cup slivered cooked ham
¼ cup sweet pickle relish
about ½ cup mayonnaise or salad
   dressing

Combine all in order, then toss gently with the mayonnaise, adding more or less according to your taste. Serve on lettuce.

Serve this excellent main-dish salad at room temperature, since much of the good cheese flavor is lost if it is chilled.

Ham Timbales with Mushroom Sauce

(Four servings)

1 cup hot milk	2 eggs, beaten
1 cup soft breadcrumbs	1 small onion, grated
pinch of salt	1 cup finely chopped cooked ham
dash of pepper	2 tablespoons melted butter or
½ teaspoon dry mustard	margarine

Combine hot milk and breadcrumbs, and stir in the salt, pepper and mustard; let stand 10 minutes. Meanwhile mix beaten eggs with onion and ham, and add melted butter. Combine with the breadcrumb mixture and pour into 4 buttered custard cups. Place cups in larger pan of hot water, bake in a 350 oven for about 40 minutes, or until timbales are set. Unmold and serve hot with Mushroom Sauce poured over each.

Timbale Mushroom Sauce

(About 1¼ cups)

2 tablespoons melted butter or	1 (4-oz.) can sliced mushrooms
margarine	milk
2 tablespoons flour	salt and pepper

Blend melted butter and flour. Reserve liquid from mushrooms and add enough milk to make 1 cup in all. Add to butter and flour, stir over low heat until smooth and thickened. Season to taste with salt and pepper, add mushrooms, and heat very hot before serving.

The Way to a Man's Vote

Over the years, women's auxiliaries in New England have made nice sums every March by serving the midday dinner at their Town Meetings. The menu was simple, but the cooking was good; and it was all clear profit, since everything was solicited. Baked beans were always served. These varied according to the recipes of the women who cooked them, but all were tasty in my home town, and some were just about the best beans ever baked.

Sometimes the political results depended upon the food. If the meal was unusually good and the men well fed, the session was apt to go smoothly, with all offices filled with great good humor and the selectmen scarcely raked over the coals at all for snowplow work during the last big storm.

However, I remember one year when H—— F——'s baked beans were the reason that the folks on the back side of town didn't get the new bridge they wanted. She was an excellent cook but always baked her beans pretty dry and not very sweet. Of course, some people like them like that.

But not Bert A——. When he sat down at the long table, he had particularly asked for good "wet" beans. But the only pot of beans left were Mrs. F——'s. Glumly, he swallowed the beans on his plate, and when he resumed his seat in the meeting, his face wore a distinctly peevish look.

When the question of voting funds to build a new bridge over

*the Hollow brook came up, he argued hotly against it, leaping to
his feet to refute every point raised. At last it was voted to "pass
over" the whole matter—the time-honored expedient used to lay a
thorny question to rest without offending either side too much.*

*I have often wondered if, after the offending beans had been
forgotten, Mr. A—— ever regretted that the bridge wasn't built.
After all, he lived on the other side of the brook, and he could
have made good use of that bridge.*

Vermont Baked Beans

(Six to eight servings)

1 pound yellow-eye or pea beans	½ teaspoon dry mustard
½ teaspoon baking soda	½ pound salt pork
1 teaspoon salt	1 small onion (optional)
½ cup maple syrup	

Cover beans with cold water and let stand overnight. In the
morning, drain and cover with fresh water. Add the soda. Cover
and simmer until beans are just tender: *don't overcook*. (A good
test is to spoon out a bean or two and blow on them; if the skin
cracks, the beans are ready.) Drain and turn into a beanpot. Add
salt, maple syrup and mustard. Some people like the flavor of
onion in their baked beans. If you do, tuck the peeled whole onion
well down into the center. Add boiling water just to the top of
the beans. Score the salt pork and place it on the surface of the
beans. Cover the pot and bake slowly in a 275 oven for at least
4 hours—you can scarcely bake beans too long, so don't worry
about them. But good baked beans should never be dry: inspect
them occasionally and add a bit of boiling water if they appear
dry.

These are the sort of beans served by the auxiliaries at our
Town Meetings. Sweetness can be regulated by the amount of
maple syrup used.

Green Beans Piquant

(Six servings)

about 5 cups cooked green beans
4 tablespoons liquid from beans
2 tablespoons melted butter or
   margarine
2 tablespoons minced onion
2 tablespoons sugar

2 tablespoons cornstarch
2 tablespoons vinegar
2 teaspoons prepared mustard
2 teaspoons prepared horseradish
2 tablespoons chopped canned
   pimiento

Reserve 4 tablespoons of the liquid when draining the beans. Simmer melted butter and onion for 5 minutes. Combine sugar and cornstarch, then blend in vinegar and the reserved bean liquid. Add to onion and butter in the frying pan and stir over low heat until smooth and thickened. Stir in mustard and horseradish, then add the pimiento. Add beans and stir to mix. Cover the pan and let stand over very low heat until all is bubbling hot, stirring occasionally to blend flavors of beans and sauce.

Kansas Corn Cakes

(Four to six servings)

2 eggs, separated
2 tablespoons flour
2 tablespoons evaporated milk
½ teaspoon salt

small pinch of pepper
2 teaspoons melted butter or
   margarine
1½ cups cooked corn, cut from cob

Beat egg yolks until light, then beat in flour, evaporated milk, salt, pepper and butter. Stir in the corn, then fold in the stiffly beaten egg whites. Drop in small spoonfuls onto a hot, greased griddle. Cook as any pancake, turning once. Serve hot with butter. Makes 12 cakes.

Tomato-Corn Pudding

(Six servings)

2 cups cream-style canned corn
1 cup canned tomatoes, undrained
1 beaten egg
¼ cup saltine crumbs
½ teaspoon seasoned salt

pinch of pepper
1 tablespoon minced onion
1 tablespoon minced green pepper
1 tablespoon melted butter or
    margarine

Combine all ingredients in order and turn into a buttered 1½-quart baking dish. Bake uncovered in a 400 oven for about 30 minutes. Remove from oven and let stand 10 minutes before serving as a side dish.

Tomato Pudding

(Four to six servings)

1 (10-oz.) can tomato purée
¼ cup boiling water
¼ teaspoon salt
¼ teaspoon basil

⅓ cup light brown sugar
2 slices soft bread, crusts removed
¼ cup melted butter or margarine

Turn the tomato purée into a pan; rinse the can with the boiling water and add. Add salt, basil and brown sugar, and bring to boiling. Cut bread in small cubes and place in a buttered baking dish. Pour the melted butter over the bread, then pour tomato mixture over all. Cover and bake in a 375 oven for about 30 minutes. Remove cover and serve hot.

Rice with Onion

(Four servings)

1 envelope dry onion-soup mix
1 cup uncooked rice

2½ cups boiling water
1 tablespoon butter or margarine

Combine ingredients in order. Turn into greased 1½-quart casserole and bake in a 375 oven for about 1 hour. Stir twice during first ½ hour of cooking time. Serve hot.

This is awfully good with roast beef or pork.

Baked Stuffed Cauliflower

(Six servings)

1 medium head cauliflower
1 cup milk
1 teaspoon dry minced onion
4 tablespoons melted butter or
    margarine
2 tablespoons flour

salt and pepper to taste
2 hard-cooked eggs, shelled and
    diced
2 tablespoons diced canned pimiento
¼ cup fine dry breadcrumbs
3 tablespoons grated sharp cheese

Trim the cauliflower and cook whole in boiling salted water for about 15 minutes or until just barely tender. Drain. Combine milk and onion. Blend 2 tablespoons of the melted butter with the flour. Add milk mixture, then stir over low heat until smooth and thick. Add salt and pepper to taste. Remove from heat and add diced eggs and pimiento. Place cauliflower head in a greased baking pan. Cut circular wedge from the center of the top and remove. Fill the cavity with part of the sauce. Replace the wedge and spoon remaining sauce over the top of the head. Combine the crumbs with the remaining 2 tablespoons melted butter and sprinkle over cauliflower. Scatter the grated cheese over all. Bake in a 375 oven until golden for about 25 minutes. Serve hot.

Such a pretty dish, and every bit as good as it is pretty!

Mushroom-Wheat Pilaf

(Four servings)

½ cup butter or margarine (1 stick)
1 small onion, peeled and diced
½ pound fresh mushrooms, sliced
1 cup bulghur (cracked wheat)

1¼ cups chicken broth
salt to taste
1 cup chopped cooked chicken or
    turkey (optional)

Melt butter in a saucepan, then add onion and mushrooms. Simmer over low heat until tender and golden brown, stirring occasionally. Add bulghur and chicken broth, cover the pan and simmer over very low heat until bulghur is tender and broth absorbed. Stir often to prevent scorching. Add salt, if needed. If desired, add chicken. Heat very hot and serve.

A tasty accompaniment to meats, and the wheat is a pleasant variation from the more usual rice. With chicken, it becomes a fine one-dish meal.

Carrots with Orange

(Three to four servings)

about 2½ cups cut-up cooked
   carrots
2 tablespoons butter or margarine
2 tablespoons sugar

¼ teaspoon grated orange rind
½ a medium orange, peeled and
   thinly sliced

Combine carrots, butter, sugar and grated orange rind in a heavy skillet. Set over low heat, cover and simmer very slowly for about 15 minutes. Stir gently several times to prevent scorching. Cut each thin orange slice in quarters and add to carrots. Mix carefully, and serve hot.

Two-Party System

There were few Democrats in town when Father was a boy but what they lacked in numbers they made up for in enthusiasm. The Democratic wives were heavily outnumbered in the kitchen when the Society prepared the noon dinner for Town Meeting, so it was thought best to ban all political talk since few women seem able to argue and work at the same time.

Sam W——was a Democrat—one of the rankest sort, his Re-

publican neighbors said. He deeply admired William Jennings Bryan, and one year had his manure-spreader drawn to one side of the town hall before March Meeting began. When the men congregated outside after the noon meal, Sam climbed on the spreader and shouted, "This is the first time I've ever spoken from a Republican platform." I doubt if many among his neighbors recognized his announcement as an outright crib from Mr. Bryan.

Old-fashioned Fried Cabbage

(Six servings)

1 medium head cabbage, shredded (about 6 cups)	1 teaspoon paprika
¼ cup margarine or butter, melted	½ cup light cream
1 teaspoon salt	1 tablespoon vinegar

Add cabbage to the melted butter in a large frying pan. Cook over low heat for about 20 minutes, stirring occasionally, adding salt and paprika after cabbage starts to simmer. When cabbage is just tender (not mushy), combine cream and vinegar and stir in gently. Serve piping hot.

An extremely good recipe from an old-time kitchen.

Deep South Candied Sweet Potatoes

(Six servings)

4 medium sweet potatoes (or yams)	1 cup undrained crushed pineapple
3 tablespoons melted butter or margarine	¼ cup light corn syrup

Cook unpeeled sweet potatoes in salted water until just tender. Drain and peel; cut in ¼-inch slices. Place slices, edges overlapping, in a buttered baking dish. Combine melted butter, pineapple and corn syrup and spoon evenly over the potato slices. Bake in a 375 oven for about 45 minutes, or until lightly browned.

Baked Turnip with Apple

(Six servings)

6 cups grated yellow turnip
1 large apple, peeled and diced
2 tablespoons light brown sugar

1 teaspoon salt
¼ teaspoon pepper
¼ cup melted butter or margarine

Combine all ingredients gently but thoroughly, and turn into a buttered 1½-quart casserole and cover. Bake in a 350 oven for about 1½ hours. Serve hot.

A fine old-fashioned vegetable as a tasty side dish.

Deviled Beets

(Six servings)

3 tablespoons melted butter or
    margarine
1 tablespoon prepared mustard
2 teaspoons vinegar

1 tablespoon honey
1 teaspoon Worcestershire sauce
½ teaspoon paprika
about 4 cups hot, sliced beets

Combine melted butter, mustard, vinegar, honey, Worcestershire sauce and paprika. Bring to boiling point, then pour over hot, well-drained beets. Stir gently to mix, and serve.

Scalloped Potatoes

(Eight servings)

6 cups pared and thinly sliced
    potatoes
1 medium onion, peeled and thinly
    sliced
2 teaspoons salt

pinch of pepper
4 tablespoons flour
3 tablespoons butter or margarine
2½ cups hot milk
paprika

Place a layer of ⅓ of the potatoes in a buttered 2-quart casserole; cover with ½ the onion slices. Combine flour, salt and pepper and sprinkle ½ the mixture over the onion layer; dot with ½ the butter. Repeat layers, ending with a potato layer. Pour hot milk over all and dust lightly with paprika. Cover and bake in a 350 oven for about 1¼ hours, or until potatoes are very tender and milk is nearly all absorbed.

Potato-Cheese Puff

(Six servings)

2 cups smoothly mashed potato
2 tablespoons melted butter or
    margarine
1 cup creamy cottage cheese
1 tablespoon grated onion

½ cup dairy soured cream
3 eggs, separated
salt and pepper to taste
paprika

With rotary beater, combine potato with the melted butter, cottage cheese, onion and soured cream. Beat in the egg yolks and add salt and pepper to taste. Beat egg whites stiff and fold in. Turn into a greased 1½-quart casserole and dust with paprika. Bake in a 350 oven for about 30 minutes, or until puffed high and golden. Serve hot.

Creamy Paprika Potatoes

(Four to six servings)

4 medium potatoes
3 tablespoons bacon or sausage fat
1½ tablespoons flour
⅔ cup hot water
1 teaspoon seasoned salt
pinch of pepper

1 small onion, minced
1 clove garlic, minced
2 teaspoons paprika
½ cup milk
4 slices crisply fried bacon, crumbled

Cut peeled potatoes in ¼-inch slices. Add to the fat melted in a frying pan and stir until potato slices are coated with the fat. Sprinkle with the flour and fry gently about 3 minutes. Add water, seasoned salt, pepper, onion and garlic. Stir to mix, cover, and simmer until potatoes are tender, about 25 minutes. Stir occasionally to prevent sticking. Sprinkle paprika over potatoes, then add the milk. Heat very hot, then serve with the crumbled bacon sprinkled over the top.

Moist and creamy, with an attractive color from the paprika. Excellent with cold meats and meat loaf.

Olive Creamed Potatoes

(Six servings)

2 cups dairy soured cream
2 tablespoons grated onion
8 finely chopped stuffed olives
½ teaspoon salt

small pinch of pepper
½ teaspoon paprika
6 medium potatoes, cooked and
cooled

Combine cream with onion, olives, salt, pepper and paprika. Heat over low flame to boiling point. Add the potatoes, peeled and cut in ½-inch cubes. Simmer over very low heat until potatoes are thoroughly hot, stirring frequently because this will scorch easily. Serve when all is well heated.

Stuffed Potato Casserole

(Six servings)

1 small onion, peeled and minced
2 tablespoons melted butter or
    margarine
1 cup dry poultry stuffing
1 egg

½ cup milk
½ teaspoon salt
pinch of pepper
2 cups seasoned mashed potato

Simmer onion in the melted butter for 5 minutes, then stir in the dry stuffing. Beat the egg with the milk, salt and pepper, blend in the mashed potatoes, then combine with the stuffing mixture. Mix well, turn into a greased 1½-quart casserole, and bake uncovered until puffed and brown, about 30 minutes, in a 375 oven.

Mighty good with meats, especially pork chops.

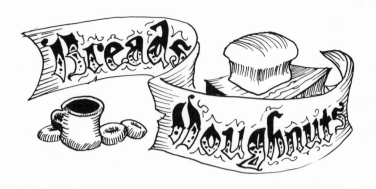

Raisin-Oatmeal Yeast Bread

(Two standard loaves)

1 cup quick oatmeal
2 cups boiling water
2 tablespoons shortening
1 tablespoon salt
½ cup honey

2 envelopes dry yeast
⅓ cup lukewarm water
about 5½ cups sifted flour
1½ cups seedless raisins

Combine oats and boiling water. Add shortening and let stand 1 hour. Stir in salt and honey. Soften yeast in the lukewarm water and add. Combine 4 cups of the flour with the raisins and add to batter. Stir in enough of the remaining flour to make a rather stiff dough; knead well on a floured board. Place in a large bowl, cover and let rise until doubled. Knead again. Shape into 2 loaves. Place in greased bread tins, cover and let rise until doubled. Bake in a 350 oven for about 50 minutes, or until bread tests done. Remove from tins to a wire rack. Brush tops with melted butter. Cool well before slicing.

Irish Potato Bread

(Two standard loaves)

1 cup leftover mashed potatoes
1 cup boiling water
2 tablespoons shortening
3 tablespoons sugar

2 teaspoons salt
1 envelope dry yeast
¼ cup lukewarm water
about 4½ cups sifted flour

Combine mashed potato and boiling water, blending well to make sure there are no lumps of potato. Add shortening and stir to melt; add sugar and salt. Cool to lukewarm. Soften yeast in the lukewarm water, add to first mixture. Stir in the flour, adding a bit more, if necessary, to make a soft, smooth dough, firm enough to be easily handled. Knead on a floured board until smooth, then place in a large bowl. Brush the top with melted shortening and cover. Let rise in warm place until doubled in bulk. Knead again and shape into 2 loaves. Place in greased bread tins, cover and let rise again until doubled. Bake in a 375 oven for about 45 minutes, or until bread tests done. Remove from tins and cool on a wire rack. Brush tops with melted butter if a soft crust is desired.

This bread keeps well without drying out.

Orange-Raisin Batter Bread

(One large round loaf)

1 cup boiling water	½ cup lukewarm water
¼ cup shortening	1 egg, beaten
½ cup sugar	2 tablespoons grated orange rind
1 teaspoon salt	1 cup seeded raisins
2 envelopes dry yeast	about 4½ cups sifted flour

Combine boiling water with shortening, sugar and salt. Stir until shortening has melted, then cool to lukewarm. Soften yeast in the lukewarm water and add to lukewarm first mixture. Add beaten egg and orange rind. Add the raisins to half the flour and stir in. Add remainder of flour to make a dough stiff enough so that it may just be turned with a heavy spoon. Cover and let rise in a warm place until doubled. Beat down with a heavy spoon, about 20 strokes. Turn into well-greased 10-inch angel cake pan and let rise again, covered, for about ½ hour. Bake in a 375 oven for about 50 minutes or until bread tests done.

May be served hot, warm or cold. Makes wonderful toast.

Onion Bread

(Two standard loaves)

1 envelope dry onion-soup mix
2 cups boiling water
3 tablespoons shortening
2 tablespoons sugar
1 teaspoon salt

3 tablespoons grated Parmesan
   cheese
1 envelope dry yeast
¼ cup lukewarm water
about 6 cups sifted flour

Combine soup mix and boiling water, cover and cook for 10 minutes. Remove from heat and add shortening, sugar and salt. Stir to melt shortening, and let stand until lukewarm. Add the cheese. Soften yeast in the lukewarm water, add to lukewarm soup mixture. Stir in flour to make a soft, yet easily handled, dough. Knead on a floured board until smooth. Place in a large bowl, cover and let rise in warm place until doubled in bulk. Knead again and shape into 2 loaves. Place in greased standard bread tins, cover and let rise again until doubled. Bake in a 375 oven for about 45 minutes, or until bread tests done. Turn out on a wire rack and brush tops with melted butter. Cool before slicing.

Makes superb sandwiches with meat or cheese.

Barmbrack

(Two tea loaves)

1 cup scalded milk
½ cup butter or margarine
3 eggs, beaten
⅔ cup sugar
1 envelope dry yeast
⅓ cup lukewarm water
about 6 cups sifted flour

1 teaspoon ground allspice
1 teaspoon salt
grated rind of 1 orange or 1 lemon
1½ cups golden raisins
½ cup candied orange or lemon
   peel

Combine hot milk and butter, stirring to melt butter, and cool to lukewarm. Stir in beaten eggs and sugar. Soften yeast in the lukewarm water, then add. Sift flour with the allspice and salt, then combine with the grated rind, raisins and candied peel. Stir into milk mixture to make a soft dough, yet stiff enough to be easily handled. (The amount of flour needed varies with the size of eggs used: the larger the eggs, the more flour.) Turn out on floured board and knead until smooth. Place in a large bowl, cover and let rise in a warm place until doubled in bulk. Knead again until smooth, then shape into 2 small loaves. Place in greased tins. Cover and let rise again until doubled. Bake in a 350 oven for about 45 minutes, or until bread tests done. Turn out on a wire rack. Brush tops wtih melted butter or margarine and sprinkle lightly with granulated sugar.

Sour Cream Crescents

(About 2 dozen)

1 cup dairy soured cream	¼ cup lukewarm water
2 tablespoons sugar	1 egg, beaten
1 teaspoon salt	about 3¼ cups sifted flour
¼ cup melted shortening	melted butter
1 envelope dry yeast	

Warm soured cream in the top pan of a double boiler. When lukewarm, remove from heat and add sugar, salt and melted shortening. Soften yeast in the lukewarm water and add. Add the beaten egg. With an electric beater, beat in 2 cups of the flour. Stir in the remaining flour to make a rather soft dough, yet stiff enough to handle. Cover and let rise in a warm place until doubled. Turn out on a floured board and knead until smooth. Divide dough in half. Pat each half into a circle about ½ inch thick and cut in about 12 wedge-shaped pieces. Brush each wedge with melted butter and roll it, beginning from wide side; pull each point and tuck it under, so the crescent will not unroll in the oven. Place on a greased pan, cover and let rise until doubled. Bake in a 375 oven for about 20 minutes.

Sally Lunn

(One 10-inch ring)

¼ cup scalded milk
⅓ cup shortening
1 envelope dry yeast
¼ cup lukewarm water

2 cups sifted flour
2 tablespoons sugar
¾ teaspoon salt
2 eggs, beaten

Stir hot milk and shortening together until shortening has melted; cool to lukewarm. Soften the yeast in lukewarm water and add to the cooled milk mixture. Sift flour with the sugar and salt, stir into the batter, then add the beaten eggs. Beat all very well, from 2 to 3 minutes. Cover and let rise in a warm place until doubled. Beat thoroughly, then turn into a greased 1½-quart ring mold. Cover and let rise again until doubled. Bake in a 400 oven for about 25 minutes. Serve hot with butter.

Classic Buttermilk Biscuits

(Sixteen average size)

2 cups flour
1 teaspoon salt
½ teaspoon baking soda

1 teaspoon baking powder
¼ cup solid shortening
¾ cup buttermilk

Sift the dry ingredients together, and rub in the shortening quickly. Add the buttermilk to make a soft dough, and turn out on a floured board. Knead lightly with a few strokes, roll out gently to ½ to ¾ inch thick. Cut into rounds and bake in a 425 oven for about 15 minutes, or until softly golden.

This is the basic rule I also like best for shortcake or cobbler or topping for some types of baked main dishes. The rule can be divided or multiplied, in which case the designation is given by the amount of flour, the other proportions remaining constant.

Feather Scones

(*About thirty*)

2 cups sifted flour	4 tablespoons softened shortening
4 teaspoons baking powder	2 eggs, beaten
⅔ teaspoon salt	about 6 tablespoons milk

Sift flour with baking powder and salt, then rub in the shortening. Beat eggs and milk together, then stir in. Use a bit more milk, if necessary, to make a rather soft yet easily handled dough. Turn out on floured board and knead slightly. Roll out to about ½ inch thick. Cut in triangles with a knife or cut with a round cutter. Place on an ungreased baking pan. Bake at 425 for about 15 minutes, or until high and brown. Serve at once with butter.

Georgia Sweet Potato Biscuits

(*About twenty*)

1¾ cups sifted flour	1 large sweet potato, peeled and
3 teaspoons baking powder	boiled
2 tablespoons sugar	⅓ cup shortening
1 teaspoon salt	¾ cup milk

Sift the flour with baking powder, sugar and salt. When the sweet potato is very tender, drain and mash it well by rubbing it through a sieve to make it very smooth. Add shortening to the hot potato and stir to melt; add milk. Combine the wet mixture with the dry mixture, stirring only enough to moisten all ingredients well. Turn out on floured board and knead lightly. Roll out to about ½ inch, cut in circles and place them on a greased pan. Bake in a 450 oven for about 20 minutes. Serve at once with butter.

Woman's World

My neighbor at the table at a recent Pancake Day in Florida was an elderly native. We had lines of communication established in no time by exchanging information about regional foods. I told her about parsnip stew and sugar-on-snow. And she spoke of the foods she knew in childhood in the piney woods of rural Florida—biscuits and sorghum three times a day, corn pones cooked in the ashes of the fireplace, turnip greens and white bacon for a treat. It was like reading The Yearling.

Cornflake Pancakes

(Twelve large cakes)

1 cup cornflakes	1 cup sifted flour
1 cup dairy soured cream	2 teaspoons baking powder
2 eggs, separated	pinch of baking soda
½ cup milk	½ teaspoon salt

Combine whole cornflakes and soured cream. Beat egg yolks lightly and add. Stir in milk. Sift flour with baking powder, baking soda and salt. Add to batter and beat well. Fold in stiffly beaten egg whites. Bake on hot greased griddle as any hotcake. Serve at once with butter and maple syrup.

Oatmeal Muffins

(One dozen)

1 cup buttermilk	½ teaspoon baking soda
1 cup quick oatmeal	2 teaspoons baking powder
½ cup light brown sugar	1 egg, beaten
1 cup sifted flour	¼ cup melted shortening
½ teaspoon salt	

Combine buttermilk, oatmeal and brown sugar, and let stand 10 minutes. Sift flour with salt, baking soda and baking powder. Add beaten egg to oatmeal mixture, then add melted shortening, mixing well. Now stir in the flour mixture, using only enough strokes to moisten all ingredients: don't beat. Fill 12 greased muffin cups. Bake in a 375 oven for about 25 minutes.

Butter Corn Sticks

(Two dozen)

⅓ cup butter or margarine
2¼ cups sifted flour
4 teaspoons baking powder
2 tablespoons sugar

1 teaspoon salt
¼ cup milk
1 cup cream-style canned corn

Melt the butter in a 13 x 9 baking pan. Sift the flour with the baking powder, sugar and salt. Stir in milk and corn. Mix, then turn out on floured board. Knead lightly, then roll to about ½ inch in thickness. Cut in 1-inch strips. Lay each strip in the melted butter, turning to coat each side. Bake in a 450 oven for about 18 minutes, or until crispy brown. Serve at once.

Steamed Boston Brown Bread

(Two loaves)

1 cup yellow cornmeal
2 cups graham flour
2 teaspoons baking soda
1 teaspoon salt

2 cups buttermilk
¾ cup light molasses
1 cup seedless raisins

Combine cornmeal, graham flour, soda and salt. Combine buttermilk, molasses and raisins. Put the two mixtures together, stirring only enough to wet all ingredients: *don't beat.* Turn into 2 greased 1-pound coffee tins. Cover tops tightly with foil. Set the cans on a rack in the steamer and steam 2 hours.

This is a traditional accompaniment to baked beans, still to be found occasionally at fund-raising suppers in place of the more usual oven-cooked loaf.

Baked Brown Bread

(One standard loaf)

1 egg, lightly beaten	½ teaspoon salt
4 tablespoons sugar	1 teaspoon baking soda
1 cup light molasses	1 cup whole wheat flour
⅔ cup buttermilk	⅔ cup seedless raisins
1 cup sifted flour	

Combine beaten egg and sugar, then blend in the molasses and stir in the buttermilk. Sift the flour with the salt and baking soda, add whole wheat flour and raisins. Combine the wet and dry mixtures, stirring only enough to wet all materials: *don't beat.* Turn into a greased standard-size bread tin and bake in a 350 oven for about 1 hour. Turn out on wire rack. Slice and serve hot.

Old-fashioned Carrot Bread

(One standard loaf)

1 cup sugar	2 teaspoons baking powder
¼ cup softened shortening	¼ teaspoon baking soda
2 eggs, to be beaten in	¾ teaspoon salt
1 cup grated raw carrots	1 cup golden raisins
grated rind 1 medium orange	½ cup chopped nuts
1½ cups sifted flour	

Cream sugar with the shortening, then beat in eggs. Beat in orange rind and grated carrots. Sift flour with baking powder, baking soda and salt. Combine with the raisins and nuts, then add to first mixture: *do not beat,* just mix enough to moisten all ingredients. Turn into a greased, standard-size bread tin (it helps in removing if the bottom of the tin is lined with greased waxed paper). Bake in a 350 oven for about 55 minutes, or until bread tests done. Let cool in the pan for 10 minutes, then turn out on a wire rack. Cool thoroughly before slicing.

Irish Tea Bread

(One standard loaf)

1 cup strong brewed tea	½ cup dried currants
1 cup light brown sugar	1 egg, beaten
1 cup seedless raisins	2 cups sifted flour
1 cup golden raisins	1 teaspoon baking powder

Combine tea, sugar, raisins and currants and let stand overnight. In the morning, stir in the beaten egg; sift the flour with the baking powder and add to the batter. Mix well but don't beat. Turn into a greased, standard-size bread tin. (If the bottom of the tin is lined with greased waxed paper, the bread will leave the tin more readily.) Bake in a 300 oven for 1 hour and 50 minutes. Turn out on a wire rack and cool thoroughly before slicing.

This is an astonishingly good bread. No salt and no fat also make this recipe a boon to those on particular diets.

Prune-Oatmeal Bread

(One standard loaf)

2 cups sifted flour	2 eggs, beaten
3 teaspoons baking powder	¼ cup vegetable oil
½ teaspoon baking soda	1 cup milk
1 teaspoon salt	1 cup chopped, pitted prunes,
¾ cup sugar	uncooked
1 cup quick oatmeal	

Sift flour with the baking powder, baking soda, salt and sugar. Stir in the oatmeal. Combine beaten eggs, oil and milk, and add to dry ingredients, stirring only enough to moisten all ingredients well. Stir in the chopped prunes and turn into greased, standard-size bread tin. Bake in a 350 oven for about 55 minutes, or until bread tests done. Turn out on a wire rack and cool well before slicing.

Cranberry-Fruit-Nut Bread

(One standard loaf)

1 cup sifted flour	1 egg, slightly beaten
1½ teaspoons baking powder	2 tablespoons melted shortening
½ teaspoon baking soda	water
½ teaspoon salt	¾ cup halved cranberries
1 cup sugar	½ cup chopped nuts
juice and grated rind of 1 medium orange	⅔ cup seedless raisins

Sift flour with baking powder, baking soda, salt and sugar. In a measuring cup, stir together the egg with the orange juice and rind and the melted shortening. Measure and add enough water to make ¾ cup of liquid. Combine wet and dry mixtures, stirring in the cranberries, nuts and raisins. Stir only enough to mix all thoroughly—don't beat—and spoon into a greased standard-size bread tin. (If you line the bottom of the tin with greased waxed paper, the loaf can be removed more easily.) Bake in a 350 oven for about 50 minutes, or until the loaf tests done. Turn out on a wire rack to cool; cool several hours before slicing.

Georgia Peanut-Banana Bread

(One standard loaf)

⅓ cup softened shortening	2 teaspoons baking powder
¾ cup chunk-style peanut butter	½ teaspoon salt
⅔ cup sugar	pinch of baking soda
2 eggs, to be beaten in	1 cup mashed bananas, very ripe
1¾ cups sifted flour	

Cream shortening with the peanut butter, then blend in the sugar and beat in the eggs thoroughly. Sift the flour with the baking powder, salt and baking soda. Add to the first mixture alternately with the mashed bananas. Mix well but don't beat. Turn into a greased, standard-size bread tin. Bake in a 350 oven for about 1 hour. Cool well on a wire rack before slicing.

Lemon Nut Bread

(One standard loaf)

⅓ cup softened shortening
1¼ cups sugar
2 eggs, to be beaten in
¼ teaspoon almond extract
1½ cups sifted flour
1 teaspoon baking powder

1 teaspoon salt
½ cup milk
1 tablespoon grated lemon rind
3 tablespoons lemon juice
⅔ cup chopped nuts

Cream shortening with the sugar, then beat in the eggs, one at a time; blend in the almond extract. Sift flour with the baking powder and salt and stir into first mixture alternately with the milk. Add the lemon rind and juice and the nuts. Do not beat, but stir only enough to moisten all ingredients thoroughly. Turn into a greased, standard-size bread tin and bake in a 350 oven for about 1 hour. Cool on a wire rack before slicing.

Light, delicately flavored, this loaf makes delightful little tea sandwiches with either butter or cream cheese.

Quick Apricot Coffeecake

(Twelve pastries)

1 package refrigerated crescent
    dinner rolls
½ cup apricot jam

1 cup dairy soured cream
1 tablespoon sugar
½ teaspoon vanilla

Unroll crescent rolls and pat into a greased 13 x 9 pan. Draw edges together with fingertips to form a sheet. Spread with the jam and bake in a 425 oven for 15 minutes. Remove from heat. Blend soured cream, sugar and vanilla smoothly and spread over the pastry. Reduce heat to 350 and return pan to oven, to bake about 5 minutes more. Serve warm, cut in squares.

Honey-Orange Nut Bread

(One standard loaf)

1 cup honey
2 tablespoons softened shortening
1 egg, to be beaten in
1 tablespoon grated orange rind
2 cups sifted flour

2 teaspoons baking powder
¼ teaspoon baking soda
½ teaspoon salt
¾ cup orange juice
¾ cup chopped nuts

Cream the honey and shortening, then beat in the egg and grated orange rind. Add to this the flour, sifted with baking powder, baking soda and salt. Add alternately with the orange juice; fold in the nuts. Mix only enough to moisten all ingredients thoroughly. Spoon into a greased, standard-size bread tin and bake about 70 minutes in a 350 oven, or until the bread tests done. Turn out on a wire rack and cool thoroughly before slicing.

Louisiana Fried Cakes

(About 3 dozen)

¾ cup scalded milk
½ cup shortening
½ cup sugar
1 teaspoon salt
1 envelope dry yeast

¼ cup lukewarm water
1 egg, beaten
about 4 cups sifted flour
1 teaspoon mace

Combine hot milk and shortening and stir until melted; add sugar and salt. Cool to lukewarm, then add the yeast, which has been softened in the lukewarm water, and the beaten egg. Sift flour with the mace and add. Add a bit more flour, if necessary, to make a soft yet easily handled dough. Knead well on a floured board, place in a bowl and cover. Let rise in a warm place until doubled. Knead again on a floured board and roll out to about ⅓ inch in thickness. Cut in 2½-inch squares. Cover and let rise until doubled. Fry in deep hot fat, 370 degrees, as for any doughnut. Drain on brown paper or paper towel. When cool dust with sugar.

Mashed Potato Doughnuts

(*About 4 dozen*)

3 tablespoons shortening	about 5 cups sifted flour
1 cup hot mashed potatoes	3 teaspoons baking powder
1 cup sugar	½ teaspoon baking soda
2 eggs, beaten	½ teaspoon salt
1 cup buttermilk	½ teaspoon nutmeg

Add shortening to hot potato and stir until melted. Cool to lukewarm, then add beaten eggs and buttermilk. Sift 3 cups of the flour with the baking powder, baking soda, salt and nutmeg. Stir into batter, then add enough of the remaining flour to make a firm dough. It should be just a bit firmer than for ordinary doughnuts. Turn out on a floured board, knead lightly, roll out and cut. Deep fry at 370 degrees.

Willie

In my Vermont hill town, Willie B—— faithfully reported at the conclusion of every food sale, supper or deer-hunters' breakfast to buy surplus doughnuts. He dearly loved the brown circles, and had found considerable difficulty in keeping supplied after his ninety-three-year-old mother died, leaving her seventy-three-year-old "boy" to manage alone.

Willie didn't mind whose doughnuts he bought, since he well knew that each one would be good. Silently, he'd indicate with a knobby finger first one doughnut, then another, always choosing the biggest. He had done this since he'd discovered that the doughnuts were exactly the same price a dozen, no matter the size.

One year he presented the Food Committee with a new doughnut cutter. Willie was quite a fair blacksmith and had, as did many another farmer, a small workshop on his place, so an outsize doughnut cutter was no problem for him at all. The committee, however, looked at the thing with considerable disfavor.

Be it known to their eternal credit that one or another of those good ladies always took her turn with the big cutter, and would bring over a dozen of the huge things, just for Willie B——'s benefit.

Whether or not he was aware of the circumstances, no one ever knew. But I'm glad to report that when the old man died a few years later, with no known kin anywhere at all, he left every dollar he possessed half to the church, half to the Ladies Aid.

Buttermilk Doughnuts

(About 3 dozen)

2 eggs, beaten
1 cup sugar
1 cup buttermilk
2 tablespoons melted shortening
3½ cups sifted flour

1 teaspoon baking powder
1 teaspoon baking soda
1 teaspoon salt
½ teaspoon nutmeg

Beat eggs and sugar together, then beat in the buttermilk and melted shortening. Sift the flour with baking powder, baking soda, salt and nutmeg and stir into the egg mixture. Mix well but don't beat. Turn out on a floured board, knead lightly, then roll out and cut. Fry in deep hot fat, 370 degrees, turning only once. Drain on brown paper or on a paper towel.

These are delicate, with a marvelous flavor.

Consumer Research

Over years of participating in putting on meals for the benefit of community enterprises in New England and the South, I have found that a 9-inch pie will serve eight (excepting, perhaps, teenage grandsons).

Of course if the pie is very rich and sweet, smaller portions are adequate, and ten pieces can be made.

Pie Pastry

(Two crusts, 9-inch)

2 cups sifted flour	⅔ cup vegetable shortening
1 teaspoon salt	about ⅓ cup ice water

Sift flour with the salt, cut in the shortening with a pastry blender until the mixture looks like coarse crumbs (or rub in with the fingers, working quickly so the shortening won't soften). Add ice water a very little at a time, using only enough to draw the dough together (too much water makes tough pastry). Turn the dough out on a lightly floured board and work gently into two balls, using only a few strokes (too much kneading also makes pastry tough). Roll each ball out to about ⅛ inch thick, allowing a good inch more in diameter than the pie pan. Use only enough flour to keep the dough from sticking to the rolling pin and board.

Halve this recipe for a 1-crust pie.

Baked Pie Shell

(Nine-inch)

Using half the recipe for Pie Pastry (two crusts), roll out about ⅛ inch thick in a circle large enough to allow a good inch of pastry to hang over the rim of the pie pan. Let the rolled pastry fall gently into the pan, being careful not to stretch it, and press it gently in place with the fingers. With fingers, turn under the overhanging edge of the pastry, and pinch it into a standing rim. Prick the pastry well over sides and bottom with a sharp fork, and bake in a 400 oven until lightly browned, about 20 minutes. Cool on a wire rack.

Patty Shells

(Six standard)

Make a full (2-cup) recipe of Pie Pastry, rolling out about ⅛ inch thick. With standard-size muffin cups as a gauge, cut 6 circles about 2 inches larger than the diameter of the cups. Place gently in each cup, taking care not to stretch it; fold and pinch a standing rim. Prick well on bottom and sides. Bake in a 400 oven for 15 to 20 minutes, or until golden. Cool on a wire rack.

Graham Cracker Crumb Crust

(One 9-inch shell)

1½ cups fine graham cracker crumbs	¼ cup sugar
	¼ cup melted butter or margarine

Combine the crumbs, sugar and melted butter. Turn into a 9-inch pie pan and press down firmly with the fingers to line the bottom and sides. Chill in the refrigerator 1 hour to firm it (otherwise it's a pan of loose crumbs), then fill. Or, if time is short, bake it for about 8 minutes in a 375 oven. Remove from oven, chill quickly, and fill.

Slipped Custard Pie

(Eight servings)

4 eggs, beaten	1 teaspoon vanilla
½ cup sugar	¼ teaspoon nutmeg
pinch of salt	baked 9-inch Pie Shell
2½ cups scalded milk	

Beat eggs, sugar, salt, milk, vanilla and nutmeg together. Butter a 9-inch pie pan liberally and pour the milk mixture into it. Set the pan in a larger pan of hot water, the depth about ½ inch. Bake in a 350 oven until the custard is firm, about 35 minutes (the custard is done when a silver knife blade comes out clean when inserted near the center). Remove the pie pan to a wire rack and cool thoroughly. A few minutes before serving time, loosen the edges of the custard carefully, using a sharp, thin knife. Hold the pan in one hand and tap lightly with other to loosen the bottom of the custard. Hold custard over the baked pie shell with both hands, the further edge of the custard over the further edge of the pie shell. Tip the custard pan and the custard will slide into place. This is easier than it sounds: in fact, I know of no one that's ever failed to do it neatly on the first try.

This is absolutely the world's best custard pie. The crust is flaky and tender, crisp and unsoaked.

Occupational Hazard

Once in a while there'd be a woman whose cooking wasn't quite up to the standards set by the rest of the Society. At one supper, Deacon S—— helped himself to a piece of Mrs. G——'s pumpkin pie, ate it, and then praised it highly. Father whispered across the table, "How in thunderation can you praise that pie?" And the deacon whispered back: "I'll tell you. It's so bad I thought it needed a few words of encouragement."

Lemon Light Bread Pie

(Six servings)

3 large slices bread, crusts removed	1 tablespoon butter or margarine
1/3 cup lemon juice	small dash of salt
2 teaspoons grated lemon rind	1/4 teaspoon cream of tartar
1 cup sugar + 6 tablespoons	8-inch baked Pie Shell, cooled
3 eggs, separated	

Dip the bread slices in hot water until well soaked, squeeze slices gently to remove excess water and combine with the lemon juice, grated rind and 1 cup of the sugar. Stir well. Add the egg yolks and beat well with a rotary beater. Place over low heat and cook, stirring constantly, until thickened. Remove from heat and add butter, stirring until melted. Cool, stirring occasionally. Spread the filling over the bottom of the pie shell. Beat the egg whites, salt and cream of tartar until stiff, then beat in the remaining 6 tablespoons of sugar very gradually, continuing until the mixture stands in peaks. Spread over the pie filling. Bake in a 325 oven for 15 to 20 minutes, or until golden brown. Cool before serving.

An absolutely delightful pie which I found in North Carolina. You'll never dream bread is one of the ingredients. This is an extremely old recipe.

High Lemon Pie

(Eight servings)

4 eggs, separated	1 envelope unflavored gelatine
3/4 cup sugar	1/4 cup cold water
1/3 cup lemon juice	1/2 teaspoon grated lemon rind
3 tablespoons orange juice	1/2 teaspoon grated orange rind
1/2 teaspoon salt	baked 9-inch Pie Shell, chilled

Beat the egg yolks until light, add ½ cup of the sugar, lemon juice, orange juice and salt and cook over low heat, stirring constantly, until smooth and thick. Add gelatine, which has been softened in the cold water, stirring to dissolve; add the grated lemon and orange rinds. Cool the mixture, then chill until partially set. Beat the egg whites until stiff, beat in the remaining ¼ cup sugar. Continue beating until stiff and glossy, fold into the gelatine mixture, and turn into the chilled pie shell. Refrigerate until firm.

Florida Orange Pie

(Eight to ten servings)

4 medium seedless oranges	unbaked 9-inch Pie Shell
1 tablespoon lemon juice	½ cup flour
grated rind of 1 orange	¼ cup sugar
1¼ cups sugar	small dash of salt
½ cup flour	2 tablespoons softened butter or
pinch of salt	margarine

Peel the oranges, removing the inner white skin. Slice thin, then combine with the lemon juice, grated rind, sugar, flour and salt. Turn into the pie shell and cover with the topping. Make topping by combining the flour, sugar and salt, then rubbing in the butter until mixture resembles coarse crumbs. Bake in a 425 oven for about 45 minutes, or until filling is golden and puffy. Cool well before serving.

Taster's Choice

One particular fund-raising endeavor of the women's auxiliaries has become increasingly popular in some areas. These events used to be billed as Nickel-a-Dip luncheons or suppers, as the case might be, but with food prices so high, they're now advertised as Dime-a-Dip. At these, the customer selects whatever she wishes to taste from the array of delectables arranged smorgas-

bord-style. Her filled plate is then checked and she is assessed ten cents for each item.

Women usually like these affairs. It's fun choosing samples of a variety of marvelous casseroles, tantalizing salads and elaborate desserts. I've never been disappointed in anything I've chosen. All have been well worth anyone's dime.

Gulf Coast Lime Pie

(Eight to ten servings)

4 eggs, separated
3 tablespoons sugar
1 cup white corn syrup
⅓ cup lime juice
1 tablespoon grated lime rind

¼ teaspoon salt
1 envelope unflavored gelatine
¼ cup cold water
baked 9-inch Pie Shell, chilled

Beat the egg yolks until fluffy, then beat in the sugar and ½ cup of the corn syrup. Add the lime juice, grated lime rind and salt, and cook over low heat, stirring constantly, until smooth and slightly thickened. Remove from heat and add the gelatine, which has been softened in the cold water, stirring until dissolved. Cool. Beat the egg whites stiff, then beat in the remaining corn syrup very gradually, beating well with a rotary beater. Fold into the lime mixture and fill the pie shell. Chill until firm.

Luscious! If desired, a few drops of green food coloring may be added to the filling.

Peach Candy Pie

(Eight servings)

4 cups sliced, peeled fresh peaches
¾ cup sugar
2 tablespoons instant tapioca
¼ cup firmly packed light brown sugar

½ cup sifted flour
4 tablespoons softened butter or margarine
unbaked 9-inch Pie Shell

Combine peaches, sugar and tapioca. Set aside while preparing pie shell. Combine the flour and brown sugar, then rub in the butter until mixture resembles coarse crumbs. Sprinkle ⅓ of the brown sugar mixture over bottom of pie shell. Turn in the peach mixture and cover with remaining brown sugar mixture. Bake in 450 oven for 10 minutes. Reduce heat to 350 and bake about 25 minutes longer or until peaches are tender and top golden. Cool well before serving.

The top is brown and sweet, the inside bright yellow and fruity.

Blue Plum Pie

(At least eight servings)

4 cups quartered pitted blue plums	½ teaspoon nutmeg
1 cup sugar	¼ cup softened butter or
¾ cup flour	margarine
¼ teaspoon salt	unbaked 9-inch Pie Shell
½ teaspoon cinnamon	

Combine the plums with ½ cup of the sugar, ¼ cup of the flour, the salt, and ¼ teaspoon each of the cinnamon and nutmeg and turn into the pie shell. Sift together the remaining ½ cup of sugar and of flour and the remaining ¼ teaspoon of cinnamon and of nutmeg. Rub in the butter until the mixture is like coarse crumbs. Spread evenly over the plums, leaving a 1-inch circle in center uncovered. Place the pie in a heavy paper bag. Fold the open end over and secure it shut with paper clips. Set the bag on a baking pan and bake in a 425 oven for 1 hour. Remove from the oven and let stand 5 minutes. Slit the bag open and remove the pie to a wire rack to cool. Serve at room temperature.

Alabama Blackberry Pie

(Eight servings)

3 cups fresh blackberries	2 tablespoons margarine or butter
1 cup sugar	¼ cup cold water
¼ cup sifted flour	Pie Pastry for 2 crusts
small dash of salt	

Turn the blackberries into a bowl. Sift sugar, flour and salt together and gently mix with the berries. Turn into a pastry-lined 9-inch pie pan. Dot with the margarine, then pour the cold water over all. Cover with the top crust, seal and crimp the edges and cut a vent in the top as usual. Bake in a 450 oven for 10 minutes; reduce heat to 375 and bake about 30 minutes longer. Cool before serving.

I bought this simple and excellent pie at a wayside food sale in Alabama, and thought it deserved mention.

Glazed Strawberry Pie

(Eight servings)

1 cup sugar	and washed
3 tablespoons cornstarch	3 drops red vegetable coloring
¼ cup cold water	(optional)
1 quart fresh strawberries, hulled	baked 9-inch Pie Shell, cooled

Combine ½ cup of the sugar with the cornstarch, blend with the cold water and add 2 cups of the strawberries, and cook over low heat until clear and thick, stirring constantly. Remove from heat and add the remaining sugar, stirring until the sugar has dissolved. Cool for 10 minutes, then add remaining 2 cups of strawberries, stirring carefully. If a deeper red color is desired, add the red coloring. Turn into the pie shell and chill for several hours before serving with any desired whipped topping.

Raspberry Dessert Pie

(Eight servings)

1 (10-oz.) package frozen
    raspberries
1 tablespoon cornstarch
baked 9-inch graham cracker crumb
    Pie Shell

½ cup lemon juice
1 (15-oz.) can sweetened *condensed*
    milk
whipped topping

Thaw the raspberries and drain, reserving the juice. Blend the cornstarch and the juice and cook over low heat until clear and thick, stirring constantly. Cool slightly, then spread in the crumb pie shell. Chill. Beat the lemon juice into the condensed milk, using a spoon to stir well. Fold in the drained berries, and carefully turn into the pie shell in a layer over the thickened juice layer. Chill. Just before serving, either whip ¾ cup heavy cream for topping or use any desired whipped topping.

Cost of Living

In these days of soaring food prices, it's imperative that each homemaker keep a wary eye on her shopping cart, weeding out the non-essentials. It is fun, as well as thrifty, to pass by glamorous ready-made food products in favor of materials that will better answer the same purpose, and with only a little more time spent in their preparation.

I recently stood at the checkout next to a young housewife who I knew was in fairly straitened circumstances. Her one cart load totaled $48.30. I could see why, when I noted the packaged cookies, the frozen meat pies, the refrigerated biscuits, the mixes of all kinds. I'd rather have seen, in her basket, cuts of cheaper meat that could have been prepared to serve several delicious meals, instead of the smaller and relatively more expensive pre-packs hardly large enough for one meal. I'd like to have seen a sack of flour, yeast cakes, raisins and spices, to make loaves of bread and dozens of cookies. I'd like to have seen a bag of pie

*apples instead of a frozen pie or two. I'd like to have seen a pack-
age of chicken wings and backs—costing less than fifty cents—
that would make many times as much good soup as she could
get from the cans of soup in her cart.*

*It seems to me that it's high time for women to free themselves
from the bondage of standardization, rigid conformity and the
dependence on packaged, dried, or frozen quick-and-easy cooking. It's time to face the fact that what is gained in convenience
they lose in individuality and in savings with good nutrition.*

Cream Cheese Date Pie

(Ten servings)

1 cup chopped pitted dates	pinch of salt
1 tablespoon grated lemon rind	2 eggs
½ cup hot water	½ cup milk
8 ounces cream cheese, softened	½ teaspoon vanilla
½ cup sugar	unbaked 9-inch Pie Shell

Combine dates, grated rind and hot water and simmer over
low heat for about 5 minutes, stirring constantly. Remove from
heat and cool. Blend cream cheese, sugar and salt. Beat in the eggs,
milk and vanilla. Beat all thoroughly, then stir in the date mixture. Turn into unbaked pie shell. Bake for 10 minutes at 425.
Reduce heat to 350 and continue baking for about 30 minutes
longer or until filling has set and is golden brown. Cool well
before serving.

Chocolate Cream Cheese Pie

(Eight to ten servings)

6 ounces semisweet chocolate bits
8 ounces cream cheese, softened
¾ cup light brown sugar, firmly
    packed
pinch of salt

1 teaspoon vanilla
2 eggs, separated
1 cup heavy cream, whipped
baked 9-inch Pie Shell

Place chocolate bits in the top of a double boiler and set over hot water. Beat cream cheese, sugar, salt and vanilla together until well blended; beat in the egg yolks, one at a time, gradually adding the melted chocolate. Beat all well, then fold in stiffly beaten egg whites, and fold in the whipped cream. Turn into the cooled pie shell. Chill in the refrigerator for several hours until firm.

A beautifully colored, rich and creamy pie.

Cherry Cheese Pie

(Ten servings)

1 cup sifted flour
3 tablespoons sugar
½ teaspoon salt
¼ cup softened butter or
    margarine

1 (1-lb.) can cherry pie filling
8 ounces cream cheese, softened
⅓ cup sugar
1 egg
1 teaspoon vanilla

Sift flour with the sugar and salt, then blend with the softened butter, and pat the mixture into a 9-inch pie pan and up the sides. Spread the cherry filling in the pastry. Bake in a 350 oven for 15 minutes. Meanwhile blend the cream cheese with the sugar, egg and vanilla, beating until thick and creamy. Remove pie from the oven, spread the cheese mixture over the cherry filling, leaving a 3-inch circle uncovered in the center. Return to the oven and bake 30 minutes longer. Cool well before serving.

Southern Peanut Butter Pie

(Ten servings)

1 cup confectioner's sugar
½ cup creamy peanut butter
3 eggs, separated
⅔ cup sugar
pinch of salt
¼ cup cornstarch

2 cups scalded milk
2 tablespoons butter or margarine
½ teaspoon vanilla
baked 9-inch Pie Shell, cooled
¼ teaspoon cream of tartar

Blend the confectioner's sugar and peanut butter together until it's a coarse crumbled mixture. Beat the egg yolks until fluffy. Combine the sugar, salt and cornstarch, beat into egg yolks; beat the hot milk in gradually. Cook over hot water until smooth and thick, stirring constantly. Remove from heat. Add the butter and vanilla. Cover the bottom of pie shell with ⅔ of the peanut butter mixture. Turn in the hot custard. Beat the egg whites until stiff with the cream of tartar. Spread them over the filling, then sprinkle the remaining ⅓ of the peanut butter mixture over the top. Bake in a 350 oven for 12 to 15 minutes, or until brown. Cool well before serving.

Raisin Meringue Pie

(Ten servings)

1½ cups seedless raisins
1½ cups water
½ cup + 4 tablespoons sugar
2 tablespoons melted butter or
    margarine
2 tablespoons flour

2 eggs, separated
1 teaspoon grated lemon rind
3 tablespoons lemon juice
baked 9-inch Pie Shell
pinch of cream of tartar

Simmer the raisins and the water until nearly tender; add ½ cup sugar and continue cooking until raisins are tender. Blend melted butter and flour. Cool ½ cup of the raisin liquid and blend with the butter mixture, then stir into the raisin and water mixture and continue cooking slowly until thickened, stirring constantly. Beat the egg yolks until light, then beat in 2 tablespoons of the hot raisin mixture; add all to remaining hot mixture; add grated lemon rind and juice. Cool, and turn into pie shell. Beat the egg whites and cream of tartar until stiff, then beat in the 4 tablespoons of sugar very gradually. Spread over the pie filling. Bake in a 350 oven for about 15 minutes, or until browned. Cool well before serving.

Christmas Pie

(Eight to ten servings)

½ cup finely chopped candied fruit	2 cups light cream
¼ cup light rum	½ cup sugar
1 envelope plain gelatine	2 eggs, separated
¼ cup cold water	9-inch baked Pie Shell, chilled

Combine candied fruit and rum; set aside. Soften the gelatine in the cold water. Combine cream and ¼ cup of the sugar and heat in a double boiler. When hot, add softened gelatine and stir until dissolved. Beat egg yolks and add the hot cream mixture gradually, stirring constantly. Set over boiling water and stir until thickened. Remove from heat, cool until slightly thickened, stirring frequently. Beat egg whites until stiff, and into them fold the remaining ¼ cup sugar. Fold the egg whites into the gelatine mixture. Chill again until nearly ready to set firmly, then fold in the candied fruit mixture and spoon into the chilled pie shell. Chill for several hours before serving.

A rich and luscious flavor combination. Either a pastry or crumb crust may be used.

Mocha Pie

(Eight servings)

4 tablespoons cornstarch
2 teaspoons cocoa
dash of salt
¾ cup sugar + 4 tablespoons
½ cup *cold* coffee

2 eggs, separated
2 cups *strong hot* coffee
1 teaspoon vanilla
¼ teaspoon cream of tartar
baked 9-inch Pie Shell, cooled

Combine the cornstarch, cocoa, salt and the ¾ cup of sugar; blend in the cold coffee, then beat the egg yolks and add. Mix well, then beat in the hot coffee. Cook over low heat, stirring constantly, until smooth and thick. Remove from heat and cool; stir in vanilla, and pour into the pie shell. Beat egg whites and cream of tartar until stiff, then gradually beat in the 4 tablespoons of sugar, continuing until the meringue stands in peaks. Spread over the pie filling and bake about 15 minutes in a 325 oven, or until browned. Cool well before serving.

Nettie Holt's Molasses-Prune Pie

(Eight servings)

½ pound dried prunes
⅔ cup prune juice
4 egg yolks
¼ cup sugar
⅓ cup light molasses

1 tablespoon lemon juice
¼ cup orange marmalade
3 tablespoons melted butter or
    margarine
pastry for 2-crust, 9-inch pie

Cook the prunes according to package directions and drain, reserving the juice. Pit the prunes and cut them up. Beat the egg yolks, then beat in the sugar, molasses and lemon juice. Stir in the chopped prunes, orange marmalade and melted butter. Turn into a pastry-lined pie pan; make a lattice top. Bake in a 450 oven for 10 minutes. Reduce heat to 375 and bake about 40 minutes longer. Cool well before serving.

This traditional pie has the authentic old-time flavor.

Sour Cream Prune Pie

(Eight servings)

3 eggs
⅔ cup light brown sugar
½ teaspoon salt
½ teaspoon grated lemon rind
1 cup dairy soured cream

1½ cups chopped cooked and
    drained prunes
2 teaspoons lemon juice
baked 9-inch Pie Shell, cooled

Beat the eggs and sugar together until fluffy; beat in the salt, grated lemon rind and soured cream, and stir in the chopped prunes. Cook over low heat, stirring constantly, until thickened. Remove from heat and add the lemon juice. Cool, then turn into the pie shell. Chill for at least 3 hours before serving. Top each portion with any desired whipped topping.

Molasses-Nut Chiffon Pie

(Eight to ten servings)

1 cup cold strong coffee
½ cup light molasses
pinch of cream of tartar
pinch of cinnamon
¼ teaspoon salt

3 eggs, separated
2 envelopes unflavored gelatine
3 tablespoons sugar
¾ cup finely chopped nuts
baked 9-inch Pie Shell, chilled

Combine ½ cup of the cold coffee with the molasses, cream of tartar, cinnamon and salt; beat well. Beat the egg yolks well, add to molasses mixture, and cook over low heat until slightly thickened, stirring constantly. Soften the gelatine in the remaining ½ cup of coffee. Stir it into the hot mixture and cook for 1 minute, stirring to dissolve gelatine. Remove from heat and cool, chilling until about the consistency of syrup. Beat the egg whites until stiff, then beat in the sugar, 1 tablespoon at a time; fold into the gelatine mixture, and fold in the nuts. Turn into the pie shell and chill until firm. Serve with a dab of whipped topping over each wedge.

Cranberry Chiffon Pie

(Eight servings)

1 envelope unflavored gelatine	2 teaspoons lemon juice
¼ cup cold water	2 egg whites
1 (1-lb.) can jellied cranberry sauce	2 tablespoons sugar
small dash of salt	baked 9-inch Pie Shell, chilled
1 teaspoon grated lemon rind	

Soften the gelatine in the cold water, then set over hot water and stir until dissolved. Add the cranberry sauce, lemon rind and juice and stir until smooth. Remove from heat and cool, then chill in the refrigerator until the mixture begins to set. Meanwhile, whip the egg whites until stiff, fold in the sugar, and fold all into the gelatine mixture. Turn into the pie shell and chill until firm. Serve with a spoonful of any desired whipped topping over each portion.

Delicate Cocoanut Pie

(Eight servings)

1 envelope plain gelatine	1 cup milk
¼ cup cold water	1 teaspoon vanilla
3 eggs, separated	1 teaspoon lemon extract
½ cup sugar	½ cup flaked cocoanut
small dash of salt	baked 9-inch Pie Shell, chilled

Soften the gelatine in the cold water. Beat the egg yolks well with the sugar and salt, then add the milk and stir over low heat until smooth and thickened. Add the gelatine and stir to dissolve. Remove from heat and cool; add the vanilla, lemon extract and cocoanut. Chill until the mixture begins to set, then fold in the stiffly beaten egg whites. Turn into the chilled pie shell and refrigerate until firm.

Chocolate Satin Icing

(About 1¼ cups)

2 ounces baking chocolate
2 tablespoons butter or margarine
¼ cup hot, strong coffee
few grains of salt

1 teaspoon vanilla
about 2 cups sifted confectioner's
   sugar

Melt chocolate in the top of a double boiler set over boiling water. Add butter and stir until blended with chocolate. Remove from heat, add the coffee, and let mixture cool. Add salt and vanilla, then stir in sugar until right consistency to spread. Makes enough for top and sides of 8 x 8 cake.

Dark and chocolate-y, and remains soft and moist until the cake is gone.

7-Minute Icing

(About 1½ cups)

1 egg white
¾ cup sugar
2½ tablespoons cold water

small dash of salt
⅛ teaspoon cream of tartar
1 teaspoon vanilla

Combine all ingredients except the vanilla in the top of a double boiler. Place over boiling water and beat constantly with a rotary beater until frosting stands in peaks, 4 to 7 minutes. Remove from heat, add vanilla and spread at once.

A satisfactory all-purpose icing. This makes enough for the top and sides of a 9-inch layer cake.

Sea Foam Frosting

(About 2 cups)

3 egg whites	small dash of salt
1½ cups firmly packed light brown sugar	⅓ cup water
	1 teaspoon vanilla

Combine all ingredients except vanilla in the top of a double boiler. Cook over boiling water, beating constantly, for about 7 minutes, or until the frosting stands in peaks. Remove from heat, add vanilla and beat 1 minute. Enough for the top and sides of two 9-inch layers.

A most satisfactory icing, glossy and smooth. I've never had a failure.

Orange Icing

(Nearly 2 cups)

3 cups sifted confectioner's sugar	1 teaspoon lemon juice
⅓ cup softened shortening	few grains of salt
¼ cup hot orange juice	

Combine ingredients and beat well with electric beater until smooth. Spread over the cooled cake.

Fruit Cocktail Cake

(Twelve servings)

2 cups sifted all-purpose flour	undrained
1 cup sugar	1 beaten egg
1 teaspoon baking soda	1 cup light brown sugar
½ teaspoon salt	½ cup chopped nuts
1 (16-oz.) can fruit cocktail,	

Sift the flour with the sugar, baking soda and salt, and stir in the fruit cocktail with its liquid. Add the beaten egg, mix well, and pour into a greased 13 x 9 cake pan. Combine brown sugar and nuts and sprinkle evenly over the surface of cake. Bake in a 350 oven for about 45 minutes. Leave in the pan while cooling. Serve just warm with any desired whipped topping as a garnish.

Delicious, easy, and so quick that I can put it together within 10 minutes.

Yellow Sheet Cake

(Fifty 2-inch squares)

1¼ cups softened vegetable shortening
3 cups + 2 tablespoons sugar
5 eggs
5½ cups sifted cake flour

2½ tablespoons baking powder
2 teaspoons salt
2½ cups milk
2 teaspoons vanilla

Blend shortening and sugar well, then beat in eggs, using an electric beater. Sift flour with baking powder and salt. Combine milk and vanilla. Add dry ingredients and liquid alternately to egg mixture, beating until smooth after each addition. Beat all about 2 minutes. Turn into a greased 12 x 20 baking pan and bake in a 350 oven for about 40 minutes, or until cake tests done. Cool in pan and ice with any desired frosting.

This is the old reliable yellow cake used by hundreds of ladies' societies all over the country.

Playing Fair

Once in a while our ladies' society puts on a Recipe Food Sale, in which each article has its rule included. I'm sure this novel approach was the brain child of some woman who yearned for particular pet recipes of her neighbors but never managed to get any.

It's a point of honor with each contributor to make sure that

her recipe is absolutely correct, with no ingredients omitted. A reluctant lady, when cornered, would give a copy of her favorite rule, slyly omitting some unnoticed but crucial ingredients. And when the thing didn't turn out at all well, she'd say: "I can't understand it! I never have a bit of trouble with it—it must be something you did wrong." This little stratagem used to be practiced more often in years past when cookbooks weren't so plentiful and easily come by.

Old-fashioned Pumpkin Fruit Cake

(Twenty servings)

¾ cup softened shortening
1 cup firmly packed light brown
    sugar
2 eggs, to be beaten in
¾ cup light molasses
¾ cup smoothly mashed cooked
    pumpkin
¾ cup buttermilk
3½ cups sifted cake flour
3 teaspoons baking powder

¼ teaspoon baking soda
1 teaspoon salt
1 teaspoon cinnamon
½ teaspoon ginger
½ teaspoon allspice
1 cup finely chopped dates
1 cup finely chopped candied fruit
⅔ cup chopped raisins
1 cup chopped nuts

Cream shortening and sugar well, then thoroughly beat in the eggs one at a time. Blend in the molasses, pumpkin and buttermilk. Sift the flour with baking powder, baking soda, salt and spices. Combine with the fruits and nuts and stir into the batter, mixing thoroughly. Turn into a greased, 10-inch tube cake pan. Bake in a 350 oven for 1 hour. Turn out on a wire rack to cool. Ice with any desired icing. I like simple Orange Icing to bring out additional flavor.

A very old and very good fruit cake.

Mincemeat Fruit Cake

(Eight to ten servings)

1 cup firmly packed light brown sugar	2 cups sifted flour
½ cup softened shortening	1 teaspoon baking soda
2 eggs, separated	1 teaspoon salt
2 cups prepared mincemeat (1-lb. jar)	1 cup chopped pitted dates
	1 cup chopped nuts

Cream the sugar with the shortening, then beat in the egg yolks and stir in the mincemeat. Sift the flour with the baking soda and salt, combine with the dates and nuts, then add to the first mixture. Fold in stiffly beaten egg whites. Turn into a large bread tin which has been greased and lined with waxed paper. Bake in a 300 oven for 1½ hours. Turn out on a wire rack and cool thoroughly before slicing. This will keep several weeks if well wrapped from the air.

Dark, moist and delicious. Instead of the traditional plum pudding, slices may be warmed in a double boiler and served with any desired pudding sauce.

Mocha Refrigerator Cake

(Ten servings)

1 commercial pound cake (*c.* 12-oz. size)	1 tablespoon powdered instant coffee
1 package instant chocolate pudding mix	1 (2-oz.) envelope whipped topping mix
	1½ cups milk

Slice the cake horizontally in 3 layers. Combine pudding mix, instant coffee, whipped topping mix and milk, and beat with a rotary beater until the mixture is thick and the right consistency to spread. Spread between layers and over the top and sides of cake. Refrigerate several hours. Serve in slices.

Remarkably easy for a Dessert affair like a benefit card party or a special committee meeting—and delicious.

Orange Cream Cake

(Sixteen servings)

2½ cups sifted cake flour
1⅔ cups sugar
3½ teaspoons baking powder
1 teaspoon salt
2 teaspoons grated orange rind
¾ cup orange juice

⅔ cup softened shortening
3 eggs
⅓ cup water
1 teaspoon almond extract
Orange Icing

Sift the flour with the sugar, baking powder and salt; add grated orange rind, orange juice and shortening. Beat for about 2 minutes with an electric beater, then add the eggs, water and almond extract. Beat 2 minutes longer. Turn into a greased and floured 13 x 9 cake pan. Bake in a 350 oven for about 45 minutes, or until cake tests done. Cool in the pan, then frost with Orange Icing.

Small Chocolate Cake

(Eight servings)

2 ounces baking chocolate
½ cup boiling water
1 cup sifted cake flour
1 cup sugar
½ teaspoon baking soda
¼ teaspoon baking powder

½ teaspoon salt
¼ cup softened vegetable shortening
¼ cup buttermilk
½ teaspoon vanilla
1 egg

Combine chocolate and boiling water and stir over very low heat until chocolate has melted. Sift flour with the sugar, baking soda, baking powder and salt; add to the cooled chocolate mixture. Add the softened shortening and beat with an electric beater for about 1 minute; add the buttermilk, vanilla and egg and beat 1 minute longer. Grease an 8 x 8 cake pan and line with waxed paper which has been lightly greased. Pour in the cake batter and bake in a 375 oven for about 40 minutes, or until cake tests done. Turn out on a wire rack and cool, then frost with any desired icing.

Angel Spongecake

(Twelve servings)

5 eggs, separated
1½ cups sugar
1½ cups sifted cake flour
½ teaspoon baking powder
¼ teaspoon salt

½ cup cold water
1 tablespoon lemon juice
¾ teaspoon cream of tartar
1 teaspoon grated lemon rind

Beat egg yolks until light, then beat in ½ cup of the sugar. Sift flour with the baking powder, salt and the remaining 1 cup of sugar. Combine lemon juice and water, then add to the egg mixture alternately with the dry ingredients. Mix thoroughly. Beat egg whites until foamy, then beat in cream of tartar and continue beating until egg whites are stiff. Fold into the batter with the grated lemon rind. Turn into an ungreased and floured 10-inch angel cake pan and bake in a 325 oven until high and brown, about 55 minutes. Remove from heat, invert pan on a wire rack and let cool, then remove the cake.

Easy Upside-down Pineapple Cake

(Sixteen servings)

¼ cup softened butter or margarine
¼ cup light brown sugar
½ cup white corn syrup

12 well-drained pineapple slices
1 package white cake mix

Blend butter, sugar and syrup and spread in a 13 x 9 pan. Arrange the pineapple slices evenly over the mixture and bake in a 375 oven for 15 minutes. Remove from the oven and cover the pineapple slices with the cake batter, which has been mixed according to package directions. Bake according to time given on package. Remove from the oven and cool for 2 minutes before turning out carefully onto a large platter.

Wonderful served either hot or cold. The syrupy glaze in the bottom of the pan never gets hard or grainy.

Fairy Gingerbread

(Six nice servings)

¼ cup sugar
¼ cup melted shortening
½ cup light molasses
1 egg, beaten
1¼ cups sifted flour

1 teaspoon baking soda
½ teaspoon salt
½ teaspoon ginger
½ teaspoon cinnamon
½ cup boiling water

Blend sugar, melted shortening and molasses, then add the beaten egg. Sift flour with the soda, salt and spices and add to first mixture, beating until smooth. Add boiling water and beat again: the batter will be very thin. Pour into a greased 8 x 8 pan. Bake in a 350 oven for about 40 minutes. Serve either warm or cold.

This is very light and delicate, especially good topped with whipped cream.

Orange Marmalade Ginger Cake

(Ten servings)

1¾ cups sifted cake flour
¾ teaspoon baking powder
½ teaspoon baking soda
½ teaspoon salt
1 teaspoon cinnamon
1 teaspoon ginger

2 tablespoons softened shortening
1 egg, beaten
½ cup molasses
1 cup orange marmalade
4 tablespoons boiling water

Beat the shortening and egg together, then beat in the molasses and stir in the marmalade. Sift the flour with the baking powder, baking soda, salt and spices and add to the marmalade mixture alternately with the boiling water. Turn into a greased, waxed-paper-lined cake tin, 9 x 9. Bake in a 350 oven for about 30 minutes. Remove from the tin and cool on a wire rack. Frost with Orange Icing.

Lighter in color and more delicate than gingerbread. And very good without icing.

Applesauce Cake with Praline Topping

(Twenty servings)

2¾ cups sifted cake flour	½ teaspoon cloves
1⅓ cups sugar	½ cup softened shortening
2 teaspoons baking powder	1 (1-lb.) can applesauce
¼ teaspoon baking soda	2 eggs, to be beaten in
½ teaspoon salt	1½ cups seedless raisins
1½ teaspoons cinnamon	

Sift flour with sugar, baking powder, baking soda, salt, cinnamon and cloves. Add shortening and applesauce. Beat with an electric beater until blended, about 2 minutes. Add the eggs and beat 1 minute longer. Stir in the raisins. Turn into a greased 13 x 9 cake pan and bake in a 350 oven for about 35 minutes, or until cake tests done. Remove from the oven and set pan on wire rack for 15 minutes. Spread cake with the Praline Topping and place under the broiler on the lowest rack for 5 minutes. Topping should be bubbling and golden brown when done. Cool the cake in the pan set on wire rack. Serve slightly warm or cold.

PRALINE TOPPING

½ cup softened butter or margarine	¼ cup undiluted evaporated milk
¾ cup firmly packed light brown sugar	¾ cup chopped nuts
	⅔ cup flaked cocoanut

Blend the butter and brown sugar well, then beat in evaporated milk. Blend thoroughly, stir in the nuts and cocoanut, and spread as directed.

Ideal for Giving

The Christmas Bazaar traditionally brings the year's fund-raising activities to a close, and reading the secretaries' reports of meetings that took place before I was born makes it apparent that handiwork then was plentiful and elaborate.

There were men's tobacco bags, made by an all-day session of the Work Committee; the material was the wrists of old kid gloves donated by members of the auxiliary. Penwipers and needle-books took up the time of yet another meeting, and used scraps of leftover silk and flannel furnished by the village dress-maker. Still being made in my youth were the hand-knitted wash-cloths turned out by the dozen. They were sure to become hard and rough after a few weeks, even when fashioned of good-quality yarn; those made from twine string—a material that cost nothing—were pure torture from start to finish.

German Sour Cream Plum Cake

(Eight servings)

½ cup softened butter or margarine
1 cup + 1 tablespoon sugar
1½ cups sifted flour
¼ teaspoon salt
½ teaspoon cinnamon

¼ teaspoon baking powder
1 (28-oz.) can purple plums,
   drained and pitted
1 cup dairy soured cream
1 beaten egg

Blend the butter and sugar well together. Sift flour with the salt, cinnamon and baking powder, and combine with butter mixture until all is crumbly. Reserve ½ cup of this, pressing the remainder into the bottom of a 9 x 9 cake pan. Cut up drained plums and spread evenly over the crumb mixture. Sprinkle with the reserved ½ cup of crumbs. Bake in a 400 oven for 15 minutes. Beat soured cream with the beaten egg and the 1 tablespoon of sugar. Remove the cake from the oven and spread the cream mixture over surface of cake and continue baking in a 350 oven for about 25 minutes, or until cake is golden brown and the topping set. Remove from the oven, cut in squares and serve warm.

A sweet, rich cake to serve with coffee.

Continuity

The women in Thetford got out a cookbook many years ago, a tiny volume of few pages. Still, it shows that good cooks and good food were in town then, even as today. One contributor had appended to her rule for ginger cookies this comment: "These will keep if you don't let the boys know where they are." Boys, too, haven't changed over the years, it seems.

Mother's Filled Cookies

(About 3 dozen)

1 cup sugar	1 teaspoon vanilla
½ cup vegetable shortening	3¼ cups sifted flour
1 egg	2 teaspoons cream of tartar
½ cup milk	1 teaspoon baking soda

Cream sugar and shortening, then beat in the egg, milk and vanilla. Sift the flour with the cream of tartar and baking soda and stir into the batter. The dough should be firm but not stiff. Roll out to about ¼ inch thick (the thinner the cookies, the more delicious) and cut in circles with a standard biscuit-cutter. Place 1 teaspoon of the filling in the center of one circle and top with another. Pinch the edges together and prick the tops with a fork. Bake 12 to 15 minutes in a 375 oven. Cool on a wire rack.

This is my mother's rule, unchanged except that she used butter for the shortening. This has been a favorite cookie of three generations of children, and remains a perennial drawing-card at our food sales.

FILLING

1 cup ground raisins	1 teaspoon flour
½ cup sugar	½ cup water

Put the raisins through the coarse knife of a food grinder, then combine with sugar, flour and water. Cook over low heat until thick, about 5 minutes—it burns easily, so watch it carefully. Cool before using.

Frosted Butterscotch Cookies

(About 4 dozen)

½ cup softened vegetable shortening
1½ cups firmly packed light brown
    sugar
2 eggs, to be beaten in
1 tablespoon vinegar + scant 1 cup
    evaporated milk

2½ cups sifted flour
1 teaspoon baking soda
½ teaspoon baking powder
¾ teaspoon salt
1 teaspoon vanilla
⅔ cup chopped nuts

Cream shortening and sugar; with rotary beater, beat in the eggs. Measure vinegar into cup and fill to the 1-cup mark with undiluted evaporated milk. Let stand 10 minutes. Sift the flour with baking soda, baking powder and salt. Add to egg mixture alternately with milk mixture. Mix well, adding vanilla. Stir in the nuts, and drop by rounded teaspoonful onto a greased cookie pan. Bake in a 350 oven for about 12 minutes. Cool on wire rack, then frost.

FROSTING

¼ pound butter or margarine
    (½ cup)

2 cups confectioner's sugar
about 2 tablespoons boiling water

Melt the butter and stir in the confectioner's sugar; add enough of the boiling water to make it right to spread—a little thinner than that used for cakes.

Fudgies

(Thirty-two squares)

1 cup less 4 teaspoons vegetable oil
¾ cup cocoa
2 eggs
2 cups sugar
2½ cups sifted flour
1 teaspoon baking soda

1 teaspoon salt
1 teaspoon vanilla
1½ cups cold water
6 ounces semisweet chocolate bits
1 cup chopped nuts

Place all ingredients in order in a large bowl, with the exception of the chocolate bits and the nuts. Beat with an electric beater until thoroughly blended. The batter will be thin. Pour into an ungreased 11 x 17 jelly-roll pan. Sprinkle with the chocolate bits and the nuts. Bake in a 350 oven for about 30 minutes. Let cool in the pan, and serve right from the pan.

This is a marvelous recipe, just about the best brownies I've ever tasted.

Filled Orange Tarts

(About 3 dozen)

2 cups sifted flour	1 egg yolk
2 tablespoons confectioner's sugar	2 teaspoons grated orange rind
¾ teaspoon salt	¼ cup orange juice
¾ cup shortening	

Sift the flour with confectioner's sugar and salt; rub in the shortening. Beat the egg yolk, grated orange rind and orange juice together; add to flour mixture to make a stiff dough. Roll out on a floured board to about ⅛ inch thick. Cut in circles with a round cutter. Place ½ teaspoon of the filling in the center of each circle; fold over and seal the edges with a fork, prick tops. Place on a greased cookie pan and bake in a 400 oven for about 10 minutes, or until lightly browned. Cool on a wire rack.

FILLING

¾ cup firmly packed light brown sugar	small dash of salt
3 ounces softened cream cheese	1 teaspoon vanilla
	½ cup cocoanut

Cream the sugar with the cheese, work in the salt and vanilla, and add the cocoanut.

Carrot-Orange Cookies

(About 4 dozen)

1 cup mashed cooked carrots
   (2 cups sliced)
1 cup sugar
1 cup softened vegetable shortening
1 tablespoon grated orange rind

½ teaspoon vanilla
1 egg
2 cups sifted flour
2 teaspoons baking powder
½ teaspoon salt

Combine carrots, sugar, shortening, grated orange rind, vanilla and the egg and beat with an electric beater until thoroughly mixed. Sift flour with the baking powder and salt; stir into the batter. Mix well. Drop by heaping teaspoonful onto a greased cookie pan. Bake in a 375 oven for about 20 minutes. Cool on a wire rack.

Quick Lemon Cookies

(About 3 dozen)

1⅔ cups sifted flour
⅔ teaspoon baking powder
pinch of salt
⅔ cup softened shortening

¾ cup sugar
1 (5½-oz.) package instant lemon
   pudding mix
2 eggs, beaten

Sift the flour with baking powder and salt. Cream shortening and sugar together well, then blend in the pudding mix. Beat eggs in well with a rotary beater, and blend in the flour mixture. Drop by heaping teaspoonful onto a greased cookie pan. Bake in a 375 oven for about 10 minutes, or until cookies are golden. Don't overbake. Cool on a wire rack.

Lemonade Drops

(About 4 dozen)

1 (6-oz.) can frozen lemonade
   concentrate
1 cup softened shortening
2 eggs

1 cup sugar
3 cups sifted flour
1 teaspoon baking soda
pinch of salt

Thaw concentrate and measure, setting aside ½ the amount for the topping. Cream the shortening and sugar together well, then thoroughly beat in the eggs. Sift the flour with baking soda and salt, and add to the egg mixture alternately with ½ the lemonade concentrate (3 ounces). Drop by teaspoonful onto a greased cookie pan. Bake in a 375 oven about 10 minutes. Take from the oven and brush the tops of the cookies with the reserved 3 ounces of lemonade concentrate and sprinkle lightly with sugar. Remove cookies to wire rack to cool.

The topping adds a most unusual touch to these delicate little cookies.

The Spirit of "Making Do"

I remember one old lady who used to contribute heavily to each bazaar, although today she would be designated "underprivileged." Of cash she had little; of materials, little more. Yet her bean bags, made of scraps of blue-and-white ticking and filled with beans from her garden, sold more readily than most of the fancier things on the tables.

She had maple sugar and syrup, made by her own efforts each spring from the maples that crowded her farm buildings. Maple cookies and maple candies, among the best I've ever tasted, she made and packed in tin cans and lard pails that were saved for her by her neighbors.

To my mind, that wonderful old lady typifies the true member of Ladies Aid, Sisterhood, Circle, Auxiliary, Benevolent Society—call it by any one of its names. Dedicated to the advancement of her community and using the means available to her, she was the living symbol of that watchword of our womenfolk down through the generations: Make Do.

Gingerbread Men

(About 15 thin men)

¼ cup vegetable shortening
½ cup light brown sugar
½ cup light molasses
about 3¼ cups sifted flour
1 teaspoon baking soda
½ teaspoon salt

1 teaspoon ginger
½ teaspoon cinnamon
¼ teaspoon cloves
5 tablespoons water
¼ cup confectioner's sugar

Blend the shortening and sugar until creamy, then beat in the molasses. Sift the flour with the baking soda, salt and spices. Add alternately to the first mixture with the water, making a very stiff dough. Roll out on a floured board, the thickness depending on how thick you want your gingerbread men. Cut to shape with a sharp knife. Bake on a greased cookie pan in a 350 oven for about 10 minutes (the time will vary according to the thickness of men). Remove from the pan at once and cool. Eyes, mouth, etc., may be drawn on the cooled figures with a toothpick dipped in a blend of ¼ cup confectioner's sugar and a little water to make a paste. This may be colored with a few drops of coloring.

These are always a great favorite at the Christmas Sale.

Peanut Chocolate Swirls

(About 3 dozen)

6 ounces semisweet chocolate bits
½ cup softened shortening
½ cup smooth peanut butter
½ cup sugar
½ cup light brown sugar, firmly

packed
1 egg
1¼ cups sifted flour
½ teaspoon baking soda
½ teaspoon salt

Melt the chocolate bits in the top of a double boiler set over hot water. Blend the shortening, peanut butter, sugar and brown sugar until smooth, add the egg, beating well. Sift the flour with the baking soda and salt. Add to batter and mix well. Turn out on a floured board and shape into a rectangle about ¼ inch thick. Cool the melted chocolate slightly and spread it over the dough. Roll carefully, as for jelly roll. Cover with a waxed paper and set in the refrigerator to chill thoroughly. Slice crosswise in ¼-inch slices. Place on a greased cookie pan and bake in a 375 oven for about 12 minutes. After taking them from the oven, let the cookies remain in the pan for 5 minutes to become firm. Remove to a wire rack to cool well before serving.

Utterly delicious. If the dough is chilled overnight, use a heated knife to slice it, since the chocolate makes a very hard layer.

Chocolate Peanut Butter Drops

(About 3 dozen)

½ cup crunchy peanut butter	½ teaspoon salt
½ cup softened shortening	¼ teaspoon cinnamon
½ cup sugar	pinch of nutmeg
1 egg	¼ cup cold water
¾ cup sifted flour	½ cup quick-cooking oatmeal
½ teaspoon baking soda	6 ounces semisweet chocolate bits

Cream peanut butter, shortening and sugar together well, and beat in the egg. Sift flour with the baking soda, salt and spices; add to egg mixture with the water. Mix thoroughly, then stir in the oatmeal and chocolate bits. Drop by teaspoonful onto greased cookie pan. Bake in a 375 oven for about 10 minutes, or until golden brown. Remove from the pan and cool on a wire rack. While still warm, sprinkle with sugar lightly.

These are very good keepers.

Peanut Butter Molasses Cookies

(About 4 dozen)

½ cup softened shortening
½ cup crunchy peanut butter
½ cup sugar
½ cup light molasses
1 egg
½ teaspoon vanilla

2 tablespoons milk
1 cup sifted flour
1 teaspoon baking powder
¼ teaspoon baking soda
½ teaspoon salt

Cream the shortening and peanut butter together well, blend in the sugar and molasses and beat in the egg and vanilla. Blend in the milk. Sift flour with baking powder, baking soda and salt, and stir into the batter, mixing well. Drop from a teaspoon onto a greased cookie pan. Bake in a 375 oven for about 10 minutes. Cool on a wire rack.

Salted Peanut Cookies

(About 4 dozen)

2 (7-oz.) packages salted Spanish
    peanuts
3 eggs
1 cup firmly packed light brown

sugar
3 tablespoons flour
¼ teaspoon baking powder
1 teaspoon vanilla

Put the peanuts, skins and all, through a food grinder, using the coarse knife. Beat the eggs and sugar together well. Sift the flour and baking powder together, then add to egg-sugar mixture. Blend in vanilla. Stir in the ground peanuts. Drop by the teaspoonful into a greased cookie pan. Bake in a 400 oven for about 10 minutes. Cool on a wire rack.

You can't know how good these are until you taste them!

Molasses Oatmeal Cookies

(About 3 dozen)

1 cup sugar
½ cup vegetable oil
2 tablespoons molasses
½ teaspoon vanilla
2 eggs
2 cups sifted flour
1½ teaspoons baking soda

¾ teaspoon salt
1 teaspoon cinnamon
½ teaspoon nutmeg
½ teaspoon ginger
2 cups quick-cooking oatmeal
¾ cup seeded raisins

Blend the sugar and oil, add molasses and vanilla, then beat in the eggs. Sift the flour with baking soda, salt and spices, combine with the oatmeal and the raisins, and add to the first mixture. Mix just enough to moisten all ingredients well. Drop from a teaspoon onto a greased cookie pan. Bake in a 400 oven for about 15 minutes, or until brown. Cool on a wire rack.

Mincemeat Oatmeal Cookies

(About 3½ dozen)

½ cup softened shortening
1 cup firmly packed light brown
    sugar
1 egg
1½ cups prepared mincemeat

1¼ cups sifted flour
¾ teaspoon baking soda
½ teaspoon salt
1½ cups quick-cooking oatmeal

Cream shortening and sugar together well, then beat in the egg; add the mincemeat, mixing thoroughly. Sift the flour with baking soda and salt; add to first mixture, then stir in the oatmeal, mixing well. Drop by tablespoonful onto a greased cookie pan. Bake in a 375 oven for about 15 minutes. Cool on wire rack.

"Thinking of You"

Sunshine baskets for shut-ins are also in the category of neighborly help. At preserving time, a woman remembers to fill a few extra jars, just to be sure of having something to contribute to various sunshine baskets throughout the year.

The contents of these baskets might be almost anything. Tiny jars of preserves, tin containers of cookies or candy, a bottle of dandelion wine made the previous spring. Or there might be such items as a cake of extra-fine homemade soap, a handkerchief with a tatted edge, or a silken sachet bag filled with dried lavender.

Molasses-Prune Squares

(Sixteen good squares)

1 egg	1 cup sifted flour
½ cup sugar	¼ teaspoon baking soda
½ cup molasses	½ teaspoon salt
⅓ cup melted shortening	1 cup quick-cooking oatmeal
⅓ pound dried prunes	

Beat the egg well, then beat in the sugar, molasses and melted shortening. Beat all well with rotary beater. Cover the prunes with boiling water and let stand 5 minutes; drain and cut up—discarding pits—and add to the batter. Sift the flour with the baking soda and salt and stir into the batter, then add the oatmeal, mixing well. Spread in a greased 9 x 9 cake pan. Bake in a 350 oven for about 30 minutes. Cool in the pan. Cut in 2¼-inch squares.

Sliced Oatmeal Macaroons

(Four dozen 3-inch cookies)

1 cup light brown sugar, firmly packed	1½ cups sifted flour
1 cup white sugar	1 teaspoon baking soda
1 cup softened shortening	1 teaspoon salt
2 eggs	1 cup grated cocoanut
1 teaspoon vanilla	3 cups quick-cooking oatmeal

Cream the brown sugar, white sugar and shortening until well blended; add eggs and beat with rotary beater until fluffy; blend in the vanilla. Sift the flour with baking soda and salt, add to the batter, then stir in the cocoanut and oatmeal, mixing well. Turn out on waxed paper and shape into 2 rolls. Wrap the rolls in waxed paper and chill well. Slice, and bake on ungreased baking pans for about 10 minutes in a 350 oven. Remove from pans carefully and cool on a wire rack.

Pineapple Crumb Squares

(Nine large squares)

¼ cup softened margarine or butter
½ cup light brown sugar, firmly packed
1 egg
½ cup sifted flour

pinch of baking soda
½ cup graham cracker crumbs
1 (8-oz.) can crushed pineapple, drained
⅓ cup chopped nuts

Blend margarine and sugar; with a rotary beater, beat in the egg. Beat all until light. Sift the flour with the baking soda and stir in. Stir in the crumbs; add pineapple and nuts. Mix well, then spread in a lightly greased 8 x 8 cake pan. Bake in a 350 oven for about 30 minutes. Cool in the pan. Cut into large squares.

War Effort

During World War II, it was felt that the refreshments for the special Work Committee should be toned down in quantity and consist of non-strategic materials, so to speak. One frugal Vermont lady went a step further when it was her turn to entertain the committee.

She set forth a platter of the reddest, juiciest apples to be found in her orchard, each polished to a ruby glow. With these, she served tumblers of clear, cold spring water. To the ladies, barely hiding their dismay, the hostess said, "It's what the Government asks us to do, you know."

Chipnut Crunchies

(About 3 dozen)

1 cup softened margarine (2 sticks)	½ cup chopped nuts
½ cup sugar	2 cups sifted flour
1 cup coarse potato-chip crumbs	

Blend the margarine well with the sugar, then add the chip crumbs and the nuts. Mix well, then add the flour. The batter will be very stiff. Pinch off small bits of the dough and form into balls about the size of a walnut, and place them on an ungreased baking pan. Gently press each ball flat with a fork dipped in flour, or the bottom of a water glass that has been dipped in sugar. Bake in a 350 oven for 18 to 20 minutes, or until lightly browned. Remove very carefully to a wire rack. Cool thoroughly before serving.

These have an unusual texture, a little like shortbread.

Cornflake-Pecan Cookies

(About 3 dozen)

½ cup sugar	2 cups sifted flour
1 cup softened shortening	¼ teaspoon salt
1 egg	½ cup coarsely crumbed cornflakes
1 teaspoon vanilla	½ cup chopped nuts

Cream sugar and shortening well, then beat in the egg and vanilla. Sift the flour with the salt and add. Add cornflake crumbs and nuts with last cupful of the flour. The batter will be quite stiff. Shape into walnut-sized balls and place on an ungreased cookie pan. Flatten each ball with a fork. Bake in a 350 oven until golden brown, about 20 minutes. Remove from the pan and cool.

Unbaked Caramel Cookies

(About 5 dozen)

2 cups sugar
¾ cup butter or margarine
1 (6-oz.) can evaporated milk,
   undiluted

1 package instant butterscotch
   pudding mix
3½ cups quick-cooking oatmeal

Combine sugar, butter and evaporated milk; stir over low heat until mixture comes to a full rolling boil. Remove from heat and add pudding mix and oatmeal. Stir thoroughly. Cool 15 minutes, then drop by rounded spoonfuls onto waxed-paper-lined cookie pans.

These are really like candy, too.

Chocolate Fruit and Nut Clusters

(About 3 dozen)

6 ounces semisweet chocolate bits
½ cup crunchy peanut butter
¾ cup chopped dates

1 teaspoon vanilla
2½ cups alphabet-type oat cereal

Melt chocolate in the top of a double boiler set over warm (not boiling) water. Stir in the peanut butter, dates, vanilla and cereal. Mix gently but thoroughly. Mixture will be quite stiff. Pack into a lightly buttered 9 x 9 cake pan, pressing down with the flat of the hand. Chill for 30 minutes. Cut in squares, using a sharp knife.

Almost a candy. Excellent.

Bridge Club Dessert

(For eight)

1 (20-oz.) can crushed pineapple
1 (3-oz.) package lemon gelatine
1⅔ cups vanilla-wafer crumbs
⅓ cup melted butter or margarine

¾ cup sugar
⅓ cup softened butter or margarine
3 eggs, separated
½ cup chopped nuts

Drain the pineapple, reserving the juice. Bring the juice to boiling point and remove from heat, add gelatine, stir to dissolve. Cool, then chill until the mixture is syrupy. Meanwhile, combine vanilla-wafer crumbs with the melted margarine. With 1 cup of the crumb mixture, cover the bottom of a 10 x 7 baking dish. Blend the sugar and softened margarine until fluffy; with a rotary beater, beat in the egg yolks. Beat thoroughly, then stir in the drained pineapple, nuts and chilled gelatine mixture. Fold in stiffly beaten egg whites. Spread over the crumb layer in baking dish and scatter the remaining crumb mixture over top. Chill until firm.

This is excellent when made the day before.

Dessert in a Hurry

(Four servings)

1 cup cooked rice, cold
1 cup well-drained canned fruit,
 chopped

1 cup whipped cream, sweetened
 to taste
½ teaspoon vanilla

Fold the rice and chopped fruit into the whipped cream, which has been flavored with the vanilla. Chill well before serving.

Mrs. Addison's Mock Strawberry Shortcake

(Eight servings)

1 (2-oz.) package whipped-topping
   mix
8 slices soft white bread

1 quart fresh strawberries, hulled
⅓ cup sugar

Prepare the whipped topping according to the package directions. Trim the crusts from the bread and fit 4 slices into an 8 x 8 baking pan. Mash the berries and mix with the sugar. Spoon half the berries over the bread in the pan. Cover with half the whipped topping. Repeat layers, ending with the topping. Chill for at least 1 hour. Cut in squares to serve.

My grandmother used to make her version of this good dessert, using heavy whipping cream.

A Penny Saved . . .

Miss R—— had a haunting fear of not "having enough to see me through," and had various ingenious ways of saving cash to "lay up" against a lean old age. She wore her rubbers over her shoes only in the wet places; when she came to a dry spot, she'd carefully take off the rubbers and carry them in her hand until she reached another puddle. When too young to know any better, I once asked her why she did that, and she said, "Well, you see, rubbers cost money. And I must save what I can to see me through."

Another of her little stratagems worked briefly. When making a trip to White River Junction on the old Boston & Maine, she'd walk the three miles to the next town before boarding the train. Then she'd buy a ticket to the station just before the Junction but fail to get off there. For a little while the conductor didn't notice this little trick; then he caught up with Miss R——. When the depot to which she had bought her fare came in sight, he kindly but firmly assisted her down the steps. I guess the five-mile walk to the Junction dampened her enthusiasm for saving, for it's said she purchased the full ticket after that.

Gingerbread Pudding

(Six servings)

2 cups scalded milk
1 cup coarse, stale gingerbread
   crumbs (*see* Cakes)
small pinch of salt
1 teaspoon grated lemon rind

2 eggs, separated
pinch of cream of tartar
6 tablespoons sugar
½ teaspoon vanilla

Combine the hot milk and crumbs; let stand 10 minutes, then stir in the salt and grated lemon rind. Beat the egg yolks well, then beat milk mixture in gradually. Turn into a buttered 1½-quart baking dish and bake in a 350 oven for 30 minutes. Remove from the oven and cover with meringue made by beating the egg whites and cream of tartar until stiff, then beating in the sugar very gradually. Spread over the surface of pudding and return to oven. Bake about 15 minutes longer, or until puffed and brown. Serve warm.

Rhubarb Cup Puddings

(For six)

1½ tablespoons softened butter or
   margarine
⅔ cup sugar
small pinch of salt
2 tablespoons flour

3 eggs, separated
1 tablespoon lemon juice
1 cup stewed rhubarb, sweetened to
   taste
½ cup milk

Cream the butter, sugar and salt, then blend in the flour. Beat in the egg yolks, then add lemon juice and rhubarb, blending well. Beat in the milk, then fold in the stiffly beaten egg whites. Pour into 6 buttered custard cups. Set the cups in pan of hot water and bake in a 325 oven for about 30 minutes, or until puffed and brown. Serve warm or cold.

You really don't need a topping since the puddings have a custardy sauce on the bottom.

Crispy Rhubarb Pudding

(Eight servings)

½ cup sugar + ¾ cup	½ teaspoon vanilla
½ cup softened butter or margarine	2 cups toast cubes (about 2 slices)
2 eggs	4 cups cornflakes
½ teaspoon nutmeg	4 cups sliced rhubarb

Cream the ½ cup sugar with the butter, then beat in the eggs, nutmeg and vanilla. Stir in the toast cubes and the cornflakes. Spread half this mixture over the bottom of a buttered 2-quart baking dish. Cover with the rhubarb, then the ¾ cup sugar, and finally with a layer of the remaining cornflake mixture. Bake in a 375 oven for about 45 minutes, or until rhubarb is tender. Serve warm with either plain or whipped cream.

Baked Coffee Custard

(Six servings)

2 eggs, beaten	1 cup cold strong coffee
small dash of salt	1 cup milk
⅓ cup sugar	½ teaspoon vanilla

Beat the eggs with the salt and sugar, then beat in the coffee, milk and vanilla. Pour into 6 buttered custard cups and set the cups in a pan of hot water. Bake in a 350 oven for about 1 hour, or until custards are set. Serve just warm or cold with a small dab of any whipped topping.

Old-fashioned Betsy Pudding

(Four to six servings)

½ cup firm jam
1 egg
2 tablespoons sugar
small pinch of salt
¼ teaspoon nutmeg

1 tablespoon melted butter or
    margarine
2 cups scalded milk
1 cup coarse stale breadcrumbs
1 teaspoon vanilla

Spread the jam over the bottom of a buttered small casserole. Beat the egg with the sugar, salt, spices and melted butter, then beat in the hot milk. Stir in the breadcrumbs and vanilla. Mix well, then pour over the jam. Bake in a 350 oven for about 40 minutes, or until puffed and brown. Serve warm or cold.

A luscious fruity sauce forms on the bottom. Strawberry jam is particularly good for this.

Seminole County Orange Dessert

(For eight)

4 medium oranges
1 cup sifted flour
2 teaspoons baking powder
¼ teaspoon salt
1½ cups sugar
2 tablespoons softened butter or

margarine
½ cup milk
1 tablespoon flour
small dash of salt
¾ cup orange juice

Peel the oranges, removing white inner skin; cut in thin slices, then halve each slice, discarding any seeds. Arrange the slices in a buttered 10 x 7 baking dish. Sift the flour with the baking powder, salt and ¾ cup of the sugar; rub in the butter, and add the milk, stirring well. Spoon this batter over the orange slices. Make a sauce by combining the remaining ¾ cup sugar, flour and salt, and mixing smoothly with the orange juice. Set over low heat and cook, stirring, until the mixture comes to a boil. Remove from heat and pour carefully over the batter and oranges in the baking dish. Bake in a 375 oven for about 50 minutes. Serve just warm, with any desired whipped topping as a garnish.

Old-fashioned Orange Cracker Pudding

(For eight)

4 cups milk	1 teaspoon grated orange rind
½ cup saltine cracker crumbs	⅓ cup orange juice
2 eggs	1 cup sugar

Combine the milk and cracker crumbs and let stand 10 minutes. Add the eggs, grated orange rind, orange juice and the sugar, beating well with a rotary beater. Pour into 8 buttered custard cups and set them in pan of hot water. Bake in a 350 oven for about 30 minutes, or until pudding is set and golden. Serve cold or slightly warm.

A delicate variety of cup custard.

Latest Thing from the City

Mrs. L——, a comparative newcomer to town, was soon catalogued as a "fancy" cook—that is, she so dressed up everything she served that the original product was sometimes hard to identify. She achieved quite a good deal of notoriety by some doughnuts she brought to the women's auxiliary food sale. They looked all right and they smelled all right. But one bite revealed the awful truth. She had flavored them heavily with vanilla. Deacon J—— took a bite and remarked in astonishment, "But vanilla's for puddings!"

She also tried out new culinary ideas on other women when they met at her house. One of the most unfortunate (one still spoken of in hushed voices) was the doughnut dessert she served the Quilt Committee. This consisted of a large doughnut split across, a pineapple slice laid between the halves, and chocolate sauce and whipped cream over all.

Baked Date Pudding with Orange Sauce

(For eight)

1 cup chopped dates	1 egg
1¾ cups boiling water	1½ cups sifted flour
½ teaspoon baking soda	1 teaspoon baking powder
2 cups sugar	¼ teaspoon salt
1 tablespoon softened butter or	1 teaspoon vanilla
margarine	½ cup chopped nuts

Combine ½ cup of the dates with 1 cup of the water and simmer for 5 minutes. Remove from heat and add soda. Cream 1 cup of the sugar with the butter, then beat in the egg. Sift the flour with the baking powder and salt, add to the egg mixture alternately with the date mixture. Blend in the vanilla, beating all well. Pour into a buttered baking dish and bake in a 350 oven for 30 minutes. Meanwhile, combine the remaining ½ cup of dates with the remaining 1 cup of sugar, the remaining ¾ cup of boiling water, and the nuts. Boil 5 minutes, then set aside. Remove the pudding from the oven and let it cool in its pan. Spoon the date-nut mixture evenly over the surface, and let stand until just barely warm. Serve with Orange Sauce.

This is a simply heavenly dessert. The touch of orange brings out the best of the dates.

Orange Sauce

⅓ cup sugar
2 tablespoons cornstarch
small dash of salt
⅓ cup light corn syrup

1 cup orange juice
1 tablespoon grated orange rind
1 tablespoon butter or margarine

Combine the sugar, cornstarch, salt and corn syrup; stir over low heat until smooth and thickened. Add orange juice, grated rind and butter and cook 1 minute longer. Remove from heat and cool. Serve either cold or slightly warm.

Fudge-Nut Pudding

(For eight)

2 tablespoons softened butter or
    margarine
1¼ cups sugar
½ cup milk
1 teaspoon vanilla
1 cup sifted flour
1 teaspoon baking powder

½ teaspoon salt
2 tablespoons cocoa + ¼ cup
½ cup chopped nuts
½ cup firmly packed light brown
    sugar
1¾ cups boiling water

Blend the butter and ¾ cup of the sugar; beat in the milk and vanilla. Sift the flour with the baking powder, salt and 2 tablespoons of the cocoa, and beat into the wet mixture. Spoon into a buttered 10 x 7 baking dish and scatter the nuts over the top. Combine the remaining ½ cup of sugar and the remaining ¼ cup of cocoa and the brown sugar; sprinkle over the batter. Pour the boiling water evenly over all, but do not stir. Bake in a 375 oven for about 30 minutes. Serve warm with any desired whipped topping.

Cranberry Surprise Pudding

(Eight servings)

2½ cups cranberries
1½ cups sugar
½ cup chopped nuts
2 eggs, beaten

1 cup sifted flour
½ cup melted butter or margarine
¼ cup milk

Spread the cranberries in the bottom of a buttered 10 x 7 baking dish and sprinkle with the nuts and ½ cup of the sugar. Beat the remaining 1 cup of sugar into the eggs, then beat in the sifted flour. Combine the melted margarine and the milk and add, beating well. Pour evenly over the cranberries, and bake in a 350 oven for about 1 hour, or until the top is golden and tests done. Serve with any whipped topping. Best served slightly warm.

The lovely cake-like top covers a rich fruity layer below.

Crispy Baked Apricots

(Six to eight servings)

¼ cup softened butter or margarine
¼ cup light brown sugar
½ teaspoon ginger
½ teaspoon allspice

2½ cups cornflakes, in coarse crumbs
1 (1-lb., 13-oz.) can apricot halves, drained

Blend the butter, sugar and spices, then combine with the corn-flake crumbs until all is like a coarse meal; reserve about ⅔ cup of this mixture. Spread remaining mixture over the bottom of a 10 x 7 baking dish, patting down firmly. Arrange apricot halves evenly over this mixture, cover with the reserved ⅔ cup crumb mixture. Bake in a 350 oven for about 30 minutes. Serve warm with plain cream.

Tips on Sandwich Making

Use bread neither too soft nor too stale.

Chilled bread slices more readily.

A light coating of softened butter will keep moist fillings from soaking into the bread.

Small sandwiches are more appealing than large ones.

Instead of 1 thick slice of meat for a sandwich, try using the same amount only in paper-thin slices.

Never make sandwiches with moist fillings very far in advance of serving time.

If making sandwiches ahead of time, wrap well in waxed paper and a slightly dampened towel, then chill.

If bread is to be rolled up with the filling, press the slices with a rolling pin before spreading, in order to prevent bread from cracking when it is rolled up.

Sandwich Variations

Open Face: Use single slices of bread. Remove the crusts and cut in circles, squares, etc. Spread with fillings and decorate with stuffed olives, pimiento bits, etc.

Fingers: Remove the crusts, spread bread with filling; put two slices together and cut in narrow (but manageable) strips.

Pinwheels: Use a loaf of unsliced bread. Remove the crusts and slice lengthwise; flatten each long slice with a rolling pin so it won't crack when rolled up. Spread with filling and roll each slice lengthwise as for jelly roll. Wrap closely in waxed paper and chill well. Cut crossways, as with a log, and serve.

Ribbon: Use a loaf of unsliced bread. Remove the crusts and slice horizontally. Spread with varied fillings and re-assemble in loaf shape. Wrap closely in waxed paper and chill well. Cut in crossways slices. Use either all white bread, or alternate slices of white and dark .

Checkerboard: Make ribbon sandwiches of alternate slices of white and dark breads. Spread one side of each ribbon slice with filling and put together so that dark and light alternate. Press each 4 slices together gently but firmly. Wrap closely in waxed paper and chill well. Slice across, so that light and dark squares appear as a checkerboard pattern.

Christmas Wreath Rounds

3 ounces soft cream cheese   minced parsley
1 tablespoon cream   pimiento
dash of salt

Blend and spread on small rounds of white bread. Edge with minced parsley, and dot a bit of red pimiento in the center.

Chicken Liver Spread

1 pound chicken livers, cooked   2 tablespoons soft butter or
2 hard-cooked eggs   margarine
2 medium onions, cut up   salt and pepper to taste

Whirl all in a blender, or put through a food mill. Wonderful on any dark bread. About 3 cups.

Cream Cheese and Clam Filling

2 (3-oz.) packages cream cheese,
    softened
1 (7-oz.) can minced clams, well
    drained
1 teaspoon onion juice
1 tablespoon mayonnaise

Blend all. Makes about 1¾ cups.

Fruited Filling

3 ounces softened cream cheese
½ cup mashed banana
⅓ cup finely chopped nuts
1 cup well-drained crushed
    pineapple

Mix all well. About 2 cups.

Salmon Spread

1 cup flaked salmon
2 tablespoons lemon juice
1 tablespoon horseradish
4 tablespoons mayonnaise
salt and pepper to taste

Mix. About 1 cup.

Cheese-Nut-Olive Spread

1 pound soft cheddar cheese
1 (5-oz.) can pecans, chopped
1 (10-oz.) bottle stuffed olives,
    chopped
6 tablespoons chutney

Blend all together. Makes about 3 cups. Wonderful on pumpernickel bread.

Candid Comment

When I was a rather new housewife, the Ladies Aid put on a reception for the new minister, for which I made sandwiches of tiny strips of bread spread with peanut butter and marshmallow (at that time considered the last word in elegance). I was so proud of my tray of little sandwiches! And I was watching anxiously to see how they went, when a big, jolly farmer came by, filling his plate with a wide assortment of good things from the table. He paused at my contribution and nudged his wife.

"Godfreys!" he said, in what he evidently considered a whisper. "Will you look at the size of them! I'd hate to have to board at her house!"

Liverwurst Spread

½ pound liverwurst, mashed
1 tablespoon mayonnaise
1½ tablespoons lemon juice

1 teaspoon onion juice
salt and pepper to taste

Blend all smoothly and use on dark breads. About 1 cup.

Shrimp Butter

1 cup chopped cooked shrimp
¼ pound soft butter or margarine

1 teaspoon lemon juice
few grains of pepper

Whirl in a blender. Any cooked fish may be used instead of the shrimp. About 1¼ cups.

More Party Sandwich Fillings

Chopped candied ginger, cream cheese, milk to moisten.

Hard-cooked eggs, minced anchovies, minced celery and mayonnaise.

Thin cucumber slices and mayonnaise on thin buttered bread.

Chopped watercress, grated onion, buttered bread.

Minced cucumbers, soured cream and capers.

Ginger marmalade and chopped nuts.

Guava jelly and cream cheese.

Cottage cheese, chopped stuffed olives, onion juice and salt.

Chopped dates, ground nuts, cream cheese and pineapple juice.

Tuna fish, dairy soured cream and sweet-pickle relish.

Deviled ham, minced pickled onions and minced olives.

Flaked lobster, horseradish, chopped chives and dairy soured cream.

Chopped walnuts, chopped raisins, chopped maraschino cherries and dairy soured cream.

Minced cucumbers, dairy soured cream and chopped hard-cooked eggs.

Minced roast pork, minced apple, a tiny dash of ground ginger and mayonnaise.

Flaked salmon, minced cucumber, onion salt and mayonnaise.

Sardines, chopped hard-cooked eggs, lemon juice, grated onion and mayonnaise.

Cream cheese and crushed pineapple.

Emergency-Shelf Tuna Filling

(About 1½ cups)

⅓ cup dried celery flakes	about ½ cup mayonnaise or salad dressing
1 tablespoon instant onion flakes	
2 tablespoons sweet pepper flakes	1 (7-oz.) can tuna, drained
¼ cup cold water	¼ teaspoon salt
1 tablespoon lemon juice	dash of pepper

Combine dried vegetable flakes and the cold water, and let stand 15 minutes. Add lemon juice, then remaining ingredients. Mix gently but thoroughly. Use additional mayonnaise if desired. Enough for 6 double sandwiches.

Picnic Filling

(For 12 big sandwiches)

1 (12-oz.) can luncheon meat
2 hard-cooked eggs
2 large canned pimientos, drained
1 (3-oz.) can pitted ripe olives,
    drained
1 tablespoon grated onion

1 tablespoon prepared mustard
1 teaspoon Worcestershire sauce
3 drops Tabasco sauce
about ⅓ cup mayonnaise or salad
    dressing

Put the meat, shelled eggs, pimientos and olives through the food grinder, using a coarse knife; combine with the remaining ingredients. Mix gently, using enough mayonnaise to make a good spreading consistency.

Ham, Cheese and Prune Sandwiches

(For four)

¾ cup ground cooked ham
¼ cup shredded sharp cheese
¼ cup minced dill pickle
about 6 tablespoons mayonnaise or

salad dressing
¼ teaspoon Worcestershire sauce
9 tenderized prunes, uncooked
4 hamburger buns, split and toasted

Combine ham, cheese, pickle, mayonnaise and Worcestershire sauce, adding a bit more mayonnaise if a moister sandwich is desired. Remove pits from the prunes and chop fine, and add to ham mixture. Spread equal amounts on 4 bun halves, then cover with other 4.

Prunes and ham are a fine flavor combination.

Corned Beef and Green Pepper Sandwich Filling

(About 1½ cups)

2 hard-cooked eggs, shelled
1 small green pepper, seeded
⅔ cup finely chopped or ground

cooked corned beef
about 1 tablespoon mayonnaise
salt and pepper to taste

Chop eggs and green pepper well and combine with the chopped corned beef. Moisten with enough mayonnaise to make it the right consistency to spread. Taste and season lightly with salt and pepper.

This is excellent on either dark breads or white. Canned corned beef may be used.

Curried Egg and Olive Sandwiches

(For six)

6 hard-cooked eggs
about ½ cup mayonnaise or creamy
   salad dressing
1 teaspoon curry powder

½ cup chopped stuffed olives
½ teaspoon seasoned salt
dash of pepper
12 slices buttered white bread

Mash the eggs with a fork, and stir with enough mayonnaise to make rather moist. Blend in the curry powder, olives, seasoned salt and the pepper. Mix well, spread on 6 slices of the bread, and cover with remaining slices.

Quick Service

When we began to have occasional "summer people" patronize our suppers, some of the ladies found them a little hard to get used to, especially those who were little accustomed to real country dishes. One summer a city man came and took his place at the long table.

The chairman of the supper committee came out of the kitchen and said to the newcomer, "Do you like baked beans?" The man said he couldn't stand them. "Do you like brown bread?" she asked. And he said he couldn't stand that, either. "Do you like rhubarb pie?" And he said he couldn't stand even the thought of one!

"In that case," she said, "you'd better call it that you've already eaten." And she gathered up his plate, knife and fork.

Hot Olive Puffs

(Thirty-two squares)

8 large slices bread, crusts removed
1 (5-oz.) can deviled meat
2 teaspoons grated onion
16 stuffed olives

2 egg whites
¼ teaspoon dry mustard
¼ cup mayonnaise or salad dressing

Toast the bread slices. Combine the deviled meat and onion and spread evenly over one side of each toast slice. Arrange the slices on a lightly buttered baking pan. Cut each olive in half and arrange 4 halves evenly on each toast slice. Beat egg whites stiff, then beat in mustard and mayonnaise. Mound evenly over each olive half. Bake in a 400 oven until topping is golden, about 12 minutes. Remove, and cut each toast slice in quarters so that you have 32 squares with an olive mound in the center of each. Serve at once.

Quick and inexpensive for any occasion, particularly as an appetizer.

Old-time Ladies Aid Coffee

(Twelve excellent cups)

1 cup regular-grind coffee
1 egg, slightly beaten
1 eggshell, crushed

few grains of salt
2 quarts cold water

Mix the coffee, beaten egg, crushed eggshell and the salt. Wet with cold water and wring out a cloth bag large enough to permit the coffee to swell until double in bulk. Place the coffee inside the bag and tie shut. Bring the 2 quarts of cold water to a full boil, and pop in the bag of coffee. Let simmer 10 minutes, pushing the bag up and down several times. Remove the bag and serve at once.

This fine coffee recipe may be doubled or tripled.

South American Hot Chocolate

(For six)

⅔ cup semisweet chocolate bits
⅔ cup hot, strong coffee

4 cups milk, scalded

Place chocolate bits in the top of a double boiler, cover and set over hot water to melt. Add the hot coffee, then place the pan over direct heat and bring to a boil. Boil 1 minute, stirring. Add the hot milk and beat with a rotary beater hard for a few seconds, or until top of liquid is frothy. Cover the pan (to prevent skin from forming) and set over hot water for about 15 minutes. Serve very hot in mugs.

Old-fashioned Lemonade

(Eight to ten servings)

6 juicy lemons
1¼ cups sugar

1½ quarts cold water

Wash lemons and cut in thin slices, saving every bit of juice but discarding the seeds. Place the slices in a bowl and cover with the sugar; let stand 20 minutes. With a potato masher, press the slices firmly but gently to extract their juice. Add the cold water and press again until the water is well flavored with the lemon. Chill. To serve, pour lemonade over ice cubes in each glass. If desired, more sugar may be added. Serve with a slice of the lemon in each glass.

Spicy Iced Tea

(Generous 3 quarts)

1 teaspoon whole cloves
1½ quarts boiling water
6 tea bags

1 cup sugar
⅔ cup bottled lemon juice
1½ quarts cold water

Combine cloves and boiling water, simmer 5 minutes. Remove from heat and immediately add the tea bags. Let stand until cool, then strain. Stir in the sugar until dissolved, then add lemon juice and cold water. Serve over ice cubes.

Cranberry Punch

(About 12 servings)

1 (1-lb.) can jellied cranberry sauce
1½ cups boiling water
¾ cup orange juice

½ cup lemon juice
3 (12-oz.) cans pale dry ginger ale

Combine cranberry sauce and boiling water and stir until the jelly has blended with the water. Strain through a wire sieve. Add orange and lemon juices and chill. Chill the ginger ale. Just before serving, combine juice mixture and ginger ale carefully in a punch bowl, with a tray of ice cubes.

Rhubarb Punch

(About 3½ quarts)

8 cups sliced, unpeeled rhubarb	6 oranges
5 cups water	3 lemons
about 2 cups sugar	1 quart pale dry ginger ale, chilled

Simmer the rhubarb in the water until it is very mushy, about 15 minutes. Strain. Measure the liquid and add ⅓ cup sugar for each cup liquid, stirring over heat until the sugar has dissolved. Cool. Add the juice of the oranges and lemons. Chill. Just before serving, add the ginger ale carefully. Serve over ice cubes.

This is awfully good. If your rhubarb is the red variety, the punch will have a lovely pink color (if it isn't, you can add a judicious drop or two of food coloring). This is the punch served for many years in our area.

Ruby Punch

(For twenty-five)

2 (46-oz.) cans pineapple-grapefruit drink	⅓ cup sugar
¼ cup red-hot cinnamon candies	4 (12-oz.) cans pale dry ginger ale, chilled

Combine 1 cup of the pineapple-grapefruit drink with the cinnamon candies and stir over low heat until the candies have dissolved. Add the sugar and stir to dissolve. Combine with the remaining pineapple-grapefruit drink. Chill well. Just before serving, add the ginger ale carefully. Serve over ice cubes.

A tangy, beautifully colored punch, much used for wedding receptions in the rural South.

Raspberry Shrub

(For thirty)

4 (10-oz.) packages frozen
   raspberries, thawed

1 cup unflavored wine vinegar
5 quarts pale dry ginger ale

Combine raspberries and vinegar, cover and let stand 24 hours. Strain, pressing all the juice from the berries. Use 2 tablespoons of the resulting syrup for each tall glass of cracked ice, and fill the glass with chilled ginger ale; stir once to mix, and serve at once.

This makes about 1 quart of syrup, which can be refrigerated in a covered jar. The shrub is a deep-red, tingly, refreshing drink, lovely in hot weather.

Sherbet Punch

(About 20 servings)

1 quart orange sherbet
2 cups orange juice
½ cup lemon juice

4 (12-oz.) cans pale dry ginger ale,
   chilled

Combine ingredients in order, stirring very gently until the sherbet melts. Pour over 1 tray of ice cubes in a punch bowl, and serve at once.

A very popular wedding punch, creamy and fruity. It can be varied by substituting pineapple sherbet and pineapple juice.

Strawberry Punch

(About 16 servings)

2 quarts strong tea, cooled
1 (6-oz.) can frozen lemonade
   concentrate

½ cup sugar
1 (10-oz.) package frozen sliced
   strawberries

Stir the tea and lemonade concentrate together. Add the sugar and strawberries, stirring to dissolve and blend well. Serve over ice cubes.

Taste Sensation

When the "summer people" became numerous in my corner of Vermont and their womenfolk enrolled in our auxiliary, refreshments took on a new tone whenever one of the newcomers was hostess. Some, in blissful ignorance, even served dishes made with an ingredient seldom met with at the society's meetings.

I remember when one such hostess served an absolutely delicious fruit cup. Elderly Miss J—— ate her serving eagerly, smacked her lips, and asked if she could please have a second helping.

To her dying day, I'm quite sure that the dear little teetotaler never suspected her lapse from grace: white wine in the fruit cup was the secret of the unequaled flavor.

Mock Rum Punch

(About 16 servings)

2 cups boiling water
1 cup sugar
2 cups strong cold tea
1 cup orange juice

⅓ cup lemon juice
1 tablespoon rum extract
1 quart ginger ale, chilled

Stir the boiling water and sugar together until sugar has dissolved. Add the tea, orange juice, lemon juice and rum extract. Stir well. Chill. Just before serving, add the ginger ale. Serve over ice cubes.

Specific information and recipes for quantity cooking can be found in bulletins obtained from your state university Extension Service. Such material can also be ordered from a list of bulletins prepared by the United States Department of Agriculture in Washington, D. C., and often your local Home Demonstration leader will be a good source of information needed for serving large groups.

Amounts for Cooking

THIS:	WILL MAKE THIS:
1 lb. apples (3 medium)	3 cups diced
1 cup dried white beans	3 cups cooked
1 slice bread	$\frac{1}{2}$ cup crumbs
1 lb. cabbage	4 cups shredded
1 lb. celery (2 small bunches)	4 cups diced
1 lb. cheddar cheese	4 cups shredded
18–20 crackers, small	1 cup crumbs
1 cup heavy cream	2 cups whipped
1 lb. unpitted dates	$1\frac{3}{4}$ cups, pitted & chopped
9 graham crackers	1 cup crumbs
1 medium lemon	$3\frac{1}{2}$ tablespoons juice
1 medium lemon	$1\frac{1}{2}$ teaspoons grated rind
1 cup macaroni, spaghetti or noodles	2 cups cooked
1 medium orange	$\frac{1}{2}$ cup juice
1 medium orange	2 teaspoons grated rind
1 lb. potatoes (4 medium)	$2\frac{1}{2}$ cups diced
1 lb. dried prunes	4 cups cooked
1 cup rice	3 cups cooked
$\frac{1}{4}$ lb. walnut meats	1 cup chopped

Equivalents

1 lb. ground beef	2 cups
1 lb. dried beans	2 cups

1 lb. cocoa	4 cups
1 lb. ground coffee	3½ cups
1 lb. cottage cheese	2 cups
1 lb. diced cooked chicken	3 cups
1 ounce chocolate	1 square
1 lb. pitted dates	2 cups
1 cup egg whites	about 8 large eggs
1 lb. flour	4 cups
1 lb. chopped nut meats	4 cups
1 lb. chopped onions	3 cups
1 lb. potatoes	3 to 4 medium
1 lb. dried prunes	2½ cups
1 lb. seedless raisins	3 cups
1 lb. seeded raisins	2½ cups
1 lb. uncooked rice	2 cups
1 lb. brown sugar	3 cups
1 lb. confectioner's sugar	3½ cups
1 lb. granulated sugar	2 cups

Substitutions

Instead of this:	Use this:
1 teaspoon baking powder	¼ teaspoon soda + ½ teaspoon cream of tartar
1 square chocolate	3 tablespoons cocoa + 1 tablespoon shortening
1 tablespoon cornstarch	2 tablespoons flour
¾ cup cracker crumbs	1 cup breadcrumbs
1 cup sour milk	1 cup sweet milk + 1 tablespoon vinegar
⅔ cup honey	1 cup sugar + ⅓ cup water
1 egg	2 egg yolks + 1 tablespoon water
few drops Tabasco	small dash of cayenne or red pepper
½ cup Tartar sauce	6 tablespoons mayonnaise + 2 tablespoons sweet pickle relish
1 cup chicken broth	1 chicken bouillon cube + 1 cup boiling water
½ lb. fresh mushrooms	4-oz. can mushrooms
1 lb. shelled shrimps	5-oz. can shrimps
1½ cups diced cooked ham	12-oz. can luncheon meat, diced
1 teaspoon allspice	½ teaspoon cinnamon + ⅛ teaspoon ground cloves